HOW TO *LEARN* COMPUTER SCIENCE

Stories, skills and superpowers

Alan J. Harrison

First published 2022

by John Catt Educational Ltd,
15 Riduna Park, Station Road,
Melton, Woodbridge IP12 1QT

Tel: +44 (0) 1394 389850
Email: enquiries@johncatt.com
Website: www.johncatt.com

ISBN: 978 1 915261 36 6

Set and designed by John Catt Educational Limited

CONTENTS

FOREWORD BY CRAIG 'N' DAVE

As Craig 'n' Dave, we are best known for our computer science videos on YouTube (youtube.com/craigndave), and the course companion Smart Revise (smartrevise. craigndave.org). A question we are frequently asked is, "how did you get into computer science in the first place?"

Some of our fondest childhood memories include typing in programs from computer magazines, debugging them, running them and then attempting to extend them. We would marvel at the wonder of making a computer do something it couldn't do before. We became overlords of our own virtual worlds. Just like today, it was a time of rapid innovation and development. These were the days before the internet, where the home PC connected to a CRT television and had at most 64k of RAM. We would travel into town to visit WHSmith where they sold the latest Codemasters game on cassette tape for £1.99. Just the right price for two boys with morsels of pocket money.

Just like science has a well-trodden path of discovery from Newton to Einstein and beyond, computer science too has its own pillars of creative minds. Babbage, Lovelace, Turing, Hopper, Berners-Lee and Dijkstra to name a few.

We are delighted to have helped with this fascinating book because Alan shares our passion for computer science and striving for the very best from our students. This shines brightly through an easily digestible exploration of the history of the subject and some of its trailblazers. Each chapter concisely describing the background to a topic you will be studying and how things came to be.

In addition, the book provides thought provoking questions for you to consider, or even to challenge your teacher! It signposts excellent resources and the very best advice to help you achieve highly in the subject.

Much like the invention of the printed circuit board in the 1930s to overcome the tyranny of wires, today we are stumbling to overcome the tyranny of transistors, preventing the development of ever faster clock speeds. Today is also a time of great innovation, where every reader has the potential to become the next great trailblazer. A pillar of our industry and our future. Will that be you?

Enjoy.

Craig Sargent & Dave Hillyard of craigndave.org

INTRODUCTION

Who is this book for?

How To Learn Computer Science is for all students of computer science, at school and university. I will illuminate the subject, explain where each topic comes from, and look at its history and links to wider culture so you can make sense of it.

I will also tackle common misconceptions: mistaken ideas about the topic that slow you down. I'll share helpful resources and further reading for greater depth, and some super study skills for that top grade. Read this book to succeed in computer science!

How should I use this book?

There are many ways:

Prepare for the course
Read this book from start to finish ahead of a computer science course, maybe in the summer before you start the GCSE or A-level. This will really boost your performance.

To boost a topic
As each chapter covers a topic (e.g. "architecture", "programming") you could tackle each chapter as you study that topic in the classroom, building on what you learn from your teacher.

As a revision resource
Read the "Explore It" section then try the tasks that follow it. Lots of activities help you remember the content, including "fertile questions" and a key concepts checklist.

As a study techniques primer
You will learn study hacks like the "pomodoro technique" for getting things done, spaced retrieval to supercharge your recall, and some top tips for use in the exam hall.

First, let's look at how to study and vital skills that you need to make the most of this book.

Study skills: the AAAA framework

We will explore good study habits, starting with a clear vision of what you want to achieve right through to developing valuable exam skills. I call this the **AAAA** framework and the four A's stand for "Aspire, Approach, Act, Assess":

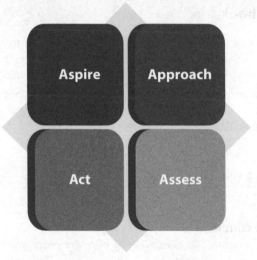

Figure 0.1: The four phases of the AAAA framework for effective study.

Aspire

A clear vision helps you achieve more. Renowned self-improvement guru Stephen Covey[1] called this "Beginning with the end in mind".

Why study computer science?
Ask yourself some questions. Why are you studying computer science? Do you need a certain grade for college? Do you want to study this subject at university or even make a career out of it? Are you studying it just for sheer enjoyment (and why not?)

The "aspire" phase asks you to explore your motivations because they will keep you going when things get tough. Studies have shown that motivated pupils work harder[2], which is not surprising really: we devote time to things we care about. Work on your motivation and you will do well.

Research careers with computing
The excellent free website **code.org** has lots of inspirational videos about careers in computer science, here link.httcs.online/codeorgcareers.

University websites are another great way to find out what you can do with computer science. The University of Manchester website explains *"Computer science helps to solve the world's greatest challenges – from medical research, education and supporting aid work in disaster areas, to the business world and visualisation, security and transmission"* (link.httcs.online/uomcareers). Decide on a career and visualise yourself doing it in five years' time!

Develop a growth mindset
You probably know about this idea, it's been pretty popular in schools in recent years. Scientists once believed that intelligence was fixed and we couldn't alter it. Now we believe that to a certain extent, everyone can improve their IQ. More importantly, with effort and motivation, you can crack any subject, if you have the right mindset.[3]

Fixed mindset	Growth mindset
I'm no good at this.	I can't do this well right now, but I can get better with practice.
I'm not a programmer.	I am not a confident programmer, but I can improve through study and practice.
Others are better than me.	Others have made more progress so far, but I can do what they did and get there too.
I make so many mistakes.	I sometimes make mistakes, but everyone does, it's all part of learning.
I've failed, I give up.	I've failed but I won't give up because the only true failure is giving up.

It's important to change your inner monologue, the voice that says, "this is too hard" and replace that negative thought with "this is tough, so I need to spend more time on it". Read *The Grit Guide for Teens* by Caren Baruch-Feldman or try some autobiographies by people who beat the odds such as Malala Yousafzai, Will Smith or Simone Biles. You could also read novels like *Wonder, Holes* or *Fish in a Tree* or watch the film *Hidden Figures*.

Try to think about your amazing abilities, not the things that hold you back. Replace "I can't do this" with "I can't do this yet, but I will" and you will see a change in your success rate. If you are are registered for the "iDea" award scheme at idea.org.uk, there is a growth mindset badge at link.httcs.online/ideagrowth and you can read more about growth mindset in the books by Carol Dweck.

"I am a programmer"

The art of programming is crucial to your success, so you need to establish early on that you are a programmer. You may think you are not, but you are, and you will be a good one before the end of the course. I know this, because I've never met a student of computer science who couldn't write a decent program by the end of the course. I'll share with you some tips, but you must own the statement "I am a programmer" and believe it!

```
coding = True
while coding:
    print("I am a programmer!")
#endwhile
```

Figure 0.2: If you write code you are a programmer!

This is the final idea in the *Aspire* principle, the idea that we can more easily form good study habits by changing our inner monologue. In his bestselling book *Atomic Habits*, James Clear explains that your current behaviours reflect your current identity. So, to become better at something, you need to start with your beliefs. If you say to yourself every day, "I am a programmer because I write programs", then becoming a better programmer is just a matter of being true to yourself and writing programs often!

Approach

OK, so now you know why you are studying this subject, you have strategies to keep you going, and you believe you are a programmer. Keep all that in mind, you'll need this amazing strength you have gained later in the course.

Now we look at the *Approach* principle which deals with how to tackle the content in the most effective way. You will need to keep your mind in top condition for learning by managing sleep, diet and stress. You need skills to stay focused and avoid distractions and boy do I have a TED talk on that! I'll show you some study techniques like the "pomodoro technique" (named after a tomato-shaped kitchen timer, but I use an app called *Forest*), and we'll learn about how the mind works which will help with understanding why this stuff is hard.

Look after your health

Getting a good night's sleep, eating well and managing anxiety are all really important. Poor sleep routines contribute to stress, heightened ADHD symptoms and poor concentration[4]. You can't study well if you didn't sleep well. Turn off devices (or lock them) at least an hour before bed and read a book instead.

Poor diet can affect your school work too, have a healthy breakfast, cut down on junk food and drink lots of water to stay alert. If you have sorted your sleep routine and diet, there is no need for caffeine-filled energy drinks which can cause insomnia, heart palpitations, obesity and diabetes.

Managing anxiety is important too. We all get anxious at times, even if you are sleeping and eating well. The pressure of exams or just that big homework deadline can get to us all, so it's important to have strategies to deal with it. When you watch the Tim Urban video in the link that follows, you'll meet the "panic monster" who arrives when a deadline is approaching to scare you into working, but keeping on top of the work helps keep anxiety away.

Taking time out to do the things that make you feel good is very important too. The word "recreation" comes from "re-creation" or making yourself new again, and you should find whatever does this for you. Find your "happy place" and go there often to ward off anxiety. But if anxiety finds you, there are things you can do. Breathing exercises are very helpful, and I find the Headspace app's guided meditation sessions very calming. Don't let anxiety get you down, take a look at the "Young Minds" website youngminds.org.uk and get some tips on beating anxiety.

Get organised

We are much better at life when we are in control. Know when your key dates are and put them on a calendar: homework, project milestones, trips and clubs. Check your calendar nightly and pack your school bag for the next day. Apart from making mornings less stressful, something rather wonderful happens in the brain when you are this organised: your subconscious does some work for you on the stuff you last thought about. You might find you wake up understanding something you were struggling with yesterday!

Make a "personal learning checklist" (see later in the book for my suggested PLCs) to keep track of your revision. Make a revision timetable in plenty of time: revising throughout the GCSE course right from the start of Year 10 is the best way, but whatever time you start, organising your study is vital.

As well as a calendar, PLC and revision timetable, make sure you keep your written notes organised. Use ring binders with dividers so you can find what you need easily. Keep your digital notes tidy too, everything in the correct folder. When studying. clear your study space and work on one thing at a time. All this organisation really improves your progress and reduces stress.

Avoid procrastination

I was going to write about this here, but I had guitar practice, a big pile of books to read and a huge Netflix queue so I ran out of time: you'll have to buy the next book to read about procrastination. Just kidding! But procrastination is a huge problem, we all have things we would rather be doing than studying. It's important to confront this issue head on, understand it, and have some strategies to deal with it.

Figure 0.3: Watch out for the instant gratification monkey, who fears nobody (except for the panic monster!)

Stop reading this book now and watch this TED talk by Tim Urban called "Inside the mind of a master procrastinator": link.httcs.online/urban. This talk explained to me why I put things off and helped me deal with the problem. Beware of the "instant gratification monkey" and take steps to keep him away! This brings me to my next tip…

Work in short, focused bursts

The "pomodoro technique" changed my life. When I had a big essay to write, like Tim Urban in that TED talk, I would see it as a huge task and put off starting it however, if you break a big task down into smaller tasks it becomes manageable: we are in the business of decomposition after all! Then allocate just 25 minutes to a task but remove all distractions and give it your full attention for the whole 25 minutes. Then allow yourself a reward. For me it's picking up my guitar or walking the dog. You choose your reward, you've worked for 25 minutes solid, you've earned it!

It's called the "pomodoro technique" because the Italian inventor used a tomato-shaped kitchen timer. But we are computer scientists, so we can go one better. Many distractions come from our smartphone, so I use the "Forest" app and "grow a tree" for 25 minutes. The app locks you out of your phone while a digital tree grows, and you can concentrate on the work. Unlock your phone and the "tree" dies! Other similar apps are available and many phones now come with wellbeing features that do similar things. Find what works for you, but as long as you find a way to focus entirely on the task in roughly 25 minute bursts, you will definitely get stuff done.

Figure 0.4: Use a timer and work in short bursts of 25 minutes without distractions.

Know your brain

In recent years, teachers have been studying what happens in the brain when we are learning. Knowing a little of how thinking works – cognitive science – will really help you understand why some things work and some don't when you are trying to learn a new subject. In summary, we only have so much "working memory": the temporary store that holds stuff we are thinking about. In computer science terms, this is like the RAM, it is limited. The brain is similar, so when we learn new stuff, we must try not to overload this working memory. We call this "reducing cognitive load".

Manage the load

Thinking is hard work. That's the key message of psychologist Daniel Willingham in his book for teachers called "Why don't students like school?"[5] But thinking hard about a subject is how we learn. So your teacher tries to make you think hard about what matters, and not waste thinking energy on stuff that doesn't matter. That useless stuff is called "extraneous cognitive load". It's like your computer having to waste RAM on things like antivirus scanning and defragging your hard drive, leaving less RAM for the good stuff like *Roblox* or *Horizon: Forbidden West.*

You can add RAM to your computer, but not to your brain, so we need some skills to reduce cognitive load:

*   Turn off your phone, put it away or at least mute it! A smartphone is a huge cognitive load-maker.

*   Tidy your workspace. Having lots of unfinished homework, books you want to read or games you want to play staring you in the face is distracting. Sure, if you share a room with others this can be tricky. But do your best to declutter.

*   One topic at a time. It's no good thinking about many subjects at once. Have a plan and work on just one thing at a time. Multitasking works for computers, but not for humans.

*   Set aside time for reading. Alan Turing's school records show that he borrowed 33 books from the school library in the three years before he left for Cambridge University. Our subject is vast and fascinating: check the appendix of this book for more computing-related literature that will amuse and astonish you.

Use your support network

This may sound obvious but talk to your teacher. If you're stuck, unsure or worried, your teacher is there for you. I'll let you into a secret, I didn't like doing this, I was embarrassed to ask for help. For that reason I nearly failed German 'O' level (that's what GCSEs were called back in the day) and actually did fail my "Mathematical Methods" exam in my first year of university. I was completely lost but didn't ask for help. When my grade came back (a "G", not even an "F") my tutor called me in and greeted me with "Alan, so nice to finally meet you, why have you not been to see me to ask for help?". I passed the resit (with help from my tutor) and the rest is history. But don't be like me, ask for help sooner!

Studying with peers is also a good idea, the gaps in your knowledge will be different, and you're actually sharing the cognitive load! And make sure you have a good textbook, either physically or digitally. I recommend the Paul Long resources to teachers, and if your school doesn't have it, you can buy access for two years as a student for £39.00 (2022 prices). We will look at other resources throughout the book.

Act

You have considered your aspirations and how to approach your studies. Now it's time to study, and what better place to start than this book? Each chapter is packed with content and solid learning activities that make a difference to your progress. You'll read a story that puts the learning in context. We explore learning hacks like retrieval practice, flashcard apps and really simple yet powerful skills like "look-say-cover-write-check". I suggest some valuable learning activities linked to each topic, with web links and apps that boost your learning. Let's look at the ideas you're going to meet in the coming pages.

Explore It

The opening section of each chapter explores the history and culture behind the topic in a "deep dive", a journey through the *core* and the *hinterland*, setting the scene and making the topic make sense. I've tried to make this a cracking read as well. There's even a *too long, didn't read* or "TL;DR" section at the end of the deep dive in case you are in a hurry!

Check It

The core concepts that you need to grasp are provided in a table called a personal learning checklist (PLC) with three columns: "need to learn", "getting there" and "mastered". As your confidence grows, tick off the next column in your PLC. Many ticks in the right column are officially a GOOD THING so aim for that.

Question It

Fertile questions – your teacher may call them "big questions" or "enquiry questions" – are what the teaching tries to answer. They are called "fertile" because they encourage you to "grow" understanding by thinking deeply about the topic. They spark your natural curiosity and give meaning to lessons.

The fertile questions appear at the start of each chapter and again throughout the deep dive, and again at the end. You think about them as you read the content, and when they come round again, your brain will be ready to "bear fruit!"

Stretch It

Learning more content helps you think more effectively about it, but thinking comes in many forms. Teachers use something called "Bloom's taxonomy of thinking skills". In rising order of difficulty, they are *remembering, understanding, applying, analysing, evaluating* and *creating*.

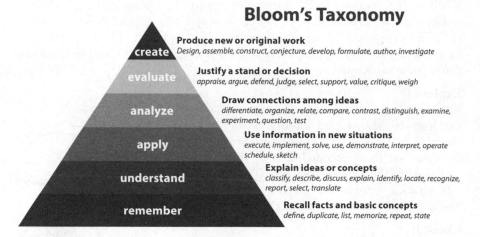

Figure 0.5: A hierarchy of thinking skills. Note: we use knowledge to create, not the other way round!

First you need to know your stuff, to remember, understand and apply the knowledge. Then you should aim to spend some time thinking at the higher levels: analysing, evaluating and creating. Some higher-order activities here will really stretch you, and if you can handle them, you clearly have mastered the topic.

Relate It

These explain abstract ideas using a similar idea in a familiar context. They help you make sense of difficult concepts.

Link It

Computer science isn't really a set of discrete topics, independent of each other. You will understand more if you make links between topics or across the curriculum, and this section includes lots of connections to get you started.

Unplug It

Getting away from the computer can help with understanding abstract concepts. We lose any distractions or technical issues. This section contains ideas for analogies, similes, metaphors, role play, games, puzzles, magic tricks and storytelling. Challenge your teacher to do one of these unplugged activities in the classroom or try them with your friends and family at home.

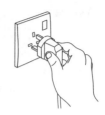

Build It

Getting hands-on can make learning computing engaging and inclusive with sensory and creative experiences. Find out what you can do with a Raspberry Pi, Micro:Bit and other equipment. Ask if you can borrow one from school or find out where your nearest Code Club or "Raspberry Jam" is happening!

Apply It

A great way to use your new-found knowledge creatively is through project work, as you apply your knowledge and make products. You get a goal, an audience and a brief to fulfil, and make your own decisions about the skills, knowledge and tools needed. Try these out in the classroom if your teacher is willing, or explore them at home, in an after-school club, Code Club or Raspberry Jam.

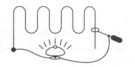

Correct It

Sometimes our ideas about the subject are wrong because we picked up false info from our daily lives or misunderstood previous lessons. Misconceptions are the enemies of progress! Each chapter lists common ones to avoid, so you don't get stuck down a dead end.

MISCONCEPTION LANE
No access to:

- Understanding Avenue
- Progress Boulevard
- Success Street

Please turn around!

Assess

The fourth "A" is "assess". Regularly review your progress to stay in control and on track. At the end of the content chapters we look at "metacognition": are your learning strategies working? What could we do better? Then it's exam technique including "command words" and the importance of SpAG. I'll also recommend some top class revision resources to ease the process.

But for now, let's explore the hinterland of the data representation topic. For this we need to head over to Switzerland, and 200 years back in time...

Note: this is not a textbook for the course. You should obtain a decent textbook as well as completing all work set by your teacher. I also recommend the videos by Craig 'n' Dave and the Isaac Computer Science website. Links to more resources can be found on my website httcs.online/learn.

Also, not wanting to clutter this book with distractions, references to academic works can all be found in my earlier book for teachers called *How to Teach Computer Science*, and are also available on my website here: httcs.online.

Endnotes

1   *The 7 Habits of Highly Effective People* by Stephen R. Covey
2   *Motivated Teaching* by Peps Mccrea
3   *Mindset: How You Can Fulfil Your Potential* by Carol Dweck
4   link.httcs.online/sleep
5   *Why Don't Students Like School?* by Daniel T. Willingham

CHAPTER 1. DATA REPRESENTATION

This topic covers how a computer stores and processes data, including binary numbers, character sets, images and sound.

Question It

Consider these now, before reading this chapter. They appear again at the end. Just take a moment to contemplate each question and think of possible answers.

1. Can a computer store and process anything we see or hear?
2. A Word document takes up just 100KB of storage until I insert images. Then it's 12MB – why?
3. JPG, GIF, SVG – why so many image file formats?
4. Why does a 700MB CD sound the same as a 50MB MP3 album?

Now read the "Explore It" discussion of the topic. You will be prompted to think about these questions again at relevant points within the text, then get a second attempt at the end of the section.

Explore It

Switzerland, June 1816

George Gordon Byron, or more popularly known as Lord Byron, has fled England and settled in Switzerland with his fellow poet Percy Bysshe Shelley and Shelley's future wife, Mary. During several days of rain, Byron suggests a competition to write the best ghost story. Mary imagines a mad professor who reanimates a corpse with tragic consequences. She names the scientist Victor Frankenstein and publishes the story anonymously on her return to England in 1818.

Byron, meanwhile, having left behind scandal, a doomed marriage, his beloved homeland and his infant daughter Augusta Ada, pens these lines:

Is thy face like thy mother's, my fair child!

Ada! sole daughter of my house and heart?

When last I saw thy young blue eyes, they smiled,

And then we parted, — not as now we part,

But with a hope. — Awaking with a start,

The waters heave around me; and on high

The winds lift up their voices: I depart,

Whither I know not; but the hour's gone by,

When Albion's lessening shores could grieve or glad mine eye.

Meeting Ada

Ada was raised by her mother, the devoutly religious and highly educated mathematician Annabella Milbanke. Byron, famously described by one of his many lovers as "mad, bad and dangerous to know", separated from Annabella after only a year of marriage, and never saw his family again. He became a hero in Greece's fight for independence from the Ottoman Empire, before dying of a fever in 1824, when Ada was eight years old.

Annabella feared Ada might inherit what she called Byron's "insanity", so she schooled Ada in science and mathematics, rather than literature. Ada's exploits brought her together with the greatest minds of the age, including Michael

Faraday, Charles Dickens and one Charles Babbage. Ada married William King, who became Earl of Lovelace, and so became the Countess of Lovelace.

Figure 1.1: Ada, Countess of Lovelace, sometimes considered the first computer programmer.

After studying birds, Ada wrote some ideas about human flight in a book she called *Flyology* at just 12 years old, showing a knack for using mathematics to understand nature. Her maths tutor, Mary Somerville – herself the first person described in print as a scientist – introduced the 17-year-old Ada to the inventor and mathematician Charles Babbage at a party where he was demonstrating his Difference Engine. Ada was fascinated by the machine and became Babbage's friend, student and assistant.

Numbers for everything

Ada saw only an unfinished prototype of the Difference Engine within her lifetime: sadly, she died of cancer in 1852, at the age of 36, while Babbage worked on an improved design for the machine. Despite this, Ada imagined a general-purpose computer that would be able to manipulate sounds and images, over 100 years before such a machine was built. In 1843, she wrote:

> *"[The Analytical Engine] might act upon other things besides number, were objects found whose mutual fundamental relations could be expressed by those of the abstract science of operations, and which should be also susceptible of adaptations to the action of the operating notation and mechanism of the engine.*

Supposing, for instance, that the fundamental relations of pitched sounds in the science of harmony and of musical composition were susceptible of such expression and adaptations, the engine might compose elaborate and scientific pieces of music of any degree of complexity or extent.[1]"

Early bitmaps

Inspired by rich, patterned fabrics called brocades, Ada also suggested a machine could create graphics. The Analytical Engine, she wrote, "weaves algebraic patterns just as the Jacquard loom weaves flowers and leaves".

By the 1840s, when Ada wrote that line, Jacquard looms were common across the UK. Rolls of punched cards drove the raising and lowering of warp threads, a difficult job previously performed by a "draw boy". A hole meant that a warp was raised; no hole left it lowered. In this way, the cards carried a binary code, read by the loom as a pattern. More than 100 years before digital computer monitors, we see a binary code that represents a two-dimensional image.

Babbage would adopt the idea of punched cards in his design for the Analytical Engine, which sadly remained unfinished. But the program that Ada designed for it, to calculate Bernoulli numbers, survived and we will look at it in chapter 5.

Figure 1.2: The Jacquard loom was fed with binary data on punched cards.

> Pause here and consider Fertile Question 1: "Can a computer store and process anything we see or hear?"
>
> _____
>
> _____

News travels slow

On the other side of the Atlantic, the problem of transcontinental communications was to drive the invention of more codes for data representation. The Gold Rush had swelled California's population to nearly 400,000 people by 1860. But they were largely cut off from the rest of the Union, with stagecoaches taking a month to make the arduous journey from east to west. With a civil war looming and local businesses demanding faster communications, a group of Missouri-based entrepreneurs founded the original Pony Express.

Using a string of 200 relief stations and lone horsemen riding in relays, the service slashed the Missouri-California mail-delivery time. In March 1861, the inaugural address of Abraham Lincoln arrived in the California capital, Sacramento, in a record seven days but the Pony Express was a flop, folding after 18 months without ever turning a profit. The route ran through Native American land, of course, and the white settlers had little respect for the native Paiute people. Frequent conflict peaked in the Pyramid Lake War in May–June 1860, in which untrained settler militias lost 80 men before the US Army arrived and killed at least 160 Paiute. But it wasn't Native American resistance that killed off the Pony Express – it was technology.

On 24 October 1861, just 17 years after Samuel Morse dispatched the first telegraphic message over his experimental line between Washington DC and Baltimore (see chapter 9), the first transcontinental telegraph line across the US was complete. Instantaneous communications rendered the Pony Express obsolete and the service closed just two days later.

Zip code

Morse's invention worked by sending pulses of electricity down cables, causing an electromagnet to raise and lower a pen that made marks on paper: the famous dots and dashes. The relay operators, however, quickly developed an ear for the clicking of the mechanism, ignoring the paper output, so Morse replaced the pen with a beeping loudspeaker. Operators would simply hear the short and long beeps and write down the English letters they represented.

A	• —	B	— • • •
C	— • — •	D	— • •
E	•	F	• • — •
G	— — •	H	• • • •
I	• •	J	• — — —
K	— • —	L	• — • •
M	— —	N	— •
O	— — —	P	• — — •
Q	— — • —	R	• — •
S	• • •	T	—
U	• • —	V	• • • —
W	• — —	X	— • • —
Y	— • — —	Z	— — • •

Figure 1.3: The Morse code table for the basic English alphabet.

Why short and long beeps? Morse had only a simple electrical circuit to play with. Either the circuit is complete, or it's not. A complete circuit would cause the speaker to beep. He realised that he could vary the duration to give himself two sounds, a short beep or "dot", and a long beep or "dash". He then assigned a set of dots and dashes to each letter of the alphabet.

Binary: yes or no?

Morse code consists of two symbols, dots and dashes, so is it a binary code? Imagine an operator needs to send the word "road". The code is dot-dash-dot pause, dash-dash-dash pause, dot-dash pause, dash-dot-dot, or • — •, — — —, • —, — • •. But if we move the last pause slightly further on in the sequence, we get "rope": • — •, — — —, • — — •, •.

> There are thousands of such ambiguous Morse patterns, including base/brie/deli, with/pens/axes, real/lend/rice and even centres/cards/trench.[2]

Clearly the gaps are significant, meaning the pauses are a symbol in their own right. In fact, a short pause is used between letters and a long pause at the end of a word, so Morse has four symbols in total: dot, dash, short pause and long pause. It's not a binary but a *quaternary* code. We need to head over to France to find an early binary code.

Bumping this one

After an accident in his father's leather workshop, Louis Braille was blind in both eyes by the age of five. At the National Institute for Blind Children in Paris some years later, Louis was shown a system of raised dots used by Napoleon's army to communicate at night. He took this system and improved upon it and by 1824, aged just 15, Louis had created a simple code of just six dots for all the letters of the alphabet, plus numbers and some punctuation symbols. Each dot is raised or flat, and a blank space separates words and sentences. In this way, the grid of six dots could represent $2 \times 2 \times 2 \times 2 \times 2 \times 2 = 2^6$ or 64 different characters.

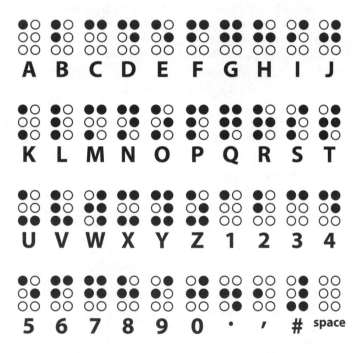

Figure 1.4: Braille is really a six-bit binary code as each of six dots is either raised or flat.

Braille is, therefore, a binary code for representing text. If we order the dots as Braille did – from 1 to 3 on the left column, top to bottom, and then 4 to 6 on the right column – then each of the braille codes can just as easily be written out as a sequence of bumps and flats. So "A" is bump-flat-flat-flat-flat-flat and "H" is bump-bump-flat-flat-bump-flat. Replacing bump with 1 and flat with 0, we can write "A" as 100000 and "H" as 110010. We can now write any text using just two digits, 0 and 1. Louis Braille had created a binary code to represent text, when electronic computers had not yet been invented.

Number crunching

The United States census surveyed over 50 million American citizens in 1880, generating a quantity of data that took almost the whole decade to process. Fearing the 1890 census wouldn't be processed before the 1900 census began, the government launched a contest for a solution.

Herman Hollerith, recalling the ticket-punch machines used by train conductors, realised that holes in card might store data readable by machines. He left his job lecturing at MIT to work for the US Patent Office in Washington DC and, in his spare time, worked on his punched card idea, winning the competition easily with a system of 24-column punched cards and tabulating machines.

Using Hollerith's machines, the 1890 "rough count" of 62 million people was announced within just six weeks, while the full reports were out in six years. Hollerith founded the Tabulating Machine Company in 1896, which would merge with other companies in the following years and by 1924 become part of International Business Machines (IBM).

Between the world wars, IBM became the largest manufacturer of electromechanical data-processing machines in the world, but they were not computers. Prongs would push through holes in card, making contact with a brush or a mercury bath on the other side, causing a mechanical adding machine – known as an accumulator – to tick over. This is where we get the word "accumulator" meaning small data store. But the machines could not run programs.

The hole truth

IBM's customers wanted to process text fields such as names and addresses, so in 1928, IBM launched the 80-column, 12-row punch-card format, creating a new binary code for representing text called Binary Coded Decimal Interchange Format (BCDIC) which later became Extended BCDIC (EBCDIC), capable of supporting many languages.

Figure 1.5 shows a Hollerith card punched with the first 64 characters of the EBCDIC character set. It was possible to punch up to 4096 different hole patterns in each column, but, in practice, punching the holes too close together broke the card, so only 256 different bit patterns were actually used.

> A card punched in every hole, known as a "lace card", was sometimes created to prank novice operators, as it would jam the card reader, needing a "card saw" to clear the blockage!

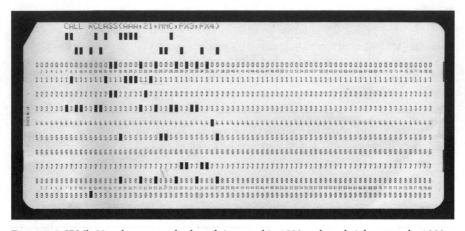

Figure 1.5: IBM's 80-column punched card, invented in 1928 and used right up to the 1980s.

Code of conduct

EBCDIC should not have been needed. In 1961, IBM engineer Bob Bemer proposed the American Standard Code for Information Interchange, or ASCII. IBM planned to adopt ASCII, but replacing all punch-card readers around the world looked too expensive, so they went with EBCDIC instead, still in use today on IBM mainframes.

EBCDIC and ASCII are character sets: look-up tables that translate letters to numeric codes. This allows computers to work with text, even text created on another computer. Most computers built after 1963, including the popular UNIVAC series, have used ASCII.

Originally a seven-bit code representing only 128 unique symbols (2^7), ASCII's international popularity demanded more characters, so an eight-bit standard called Extended ASCII emerged in 1987. Sharing a character set paved the way for direct networked communications, beginning with the ARPANET project in 1969, which had developed into the modern internet by 1981 (see chapter 9). The internet would not have been possible without ASCII.

Eight bits is not enough

256 different bit patterns available from eight bits (2^8) were not enough for languages such as Arabic, Chinese and Japanese, and the Unicode standard was created in 1991. Originally a 16-bit code, a later version called UTF-8 allowed up to 32 bits per character, giving room for all modern languages. The first 128 characters of UTF-8 are identical to ASCII, making it backwards-compatible.

As Unicode opened the internet to non-English-speaking peoples, the universal character set was an important leveller. Unicode lawyer Andy Updegrove explained in a 2015 interview, "Without [Unicode] we would be stuck in an upgraded example of a colonial world, where historically first world nations continue to force their cultures and rules on emerging nations and their peoples."[3]

Pause here and consider Fertile Question 2: "What would a world without character sets like ASCII and Unicode look like?"

_____

_____

Just the fax, ma'am

Taking a selfie with a modern smartphone and sending it to friends has become second nature to us. Finnish mobile giant Nokia released the 7650 with a 104 MHz RISC device complete with a 0.3-megapixel camera in 2001 and sold 750,000 every month during 2002. What these early "cameraphone" owners didn't know was that digital images were being transmitted across the world more than 130 years earlier.

The Scottish inventor and clockmaker Alexander Bain devised an experimental "facsimile" machine in 1846. The results were disappointing because it was hard to synchronise the machines at each end, but the principle was sound. Building on Bain's work, the Italian physicist Giovanni Caselli successfully launched the first commercial fax service between Paris and Lyon in 1865. In 1921, the first newspaper images were successfully transmitted by submarine cable from London to New York. The "Bartlane" system used a five-hole paper tape, each column using a 5-bit binary code to represent the brightness of a "pixel" rendered in greyscale by the receiving printer.[4]

These early image-encoding techniques were invented to transmit pictures over distance, but they all used a binary code to represent real-world data. Once the digital computer age was upon us, the challenge became simply how to store these black and white or greyscale brightness values and process them electronically. In 1948, scientists at Manchester University did just that.

Family album

An early computer called the Manchester Baby was invented by Freddie Williams and Tom Kilburn at Manchester University in the 1940s (see chapter 6). The machine used a cathode ray tube (CRT) for memory, wired to self-refresh every millisecond so it didn't forget its contents. Each dot on the phosphor screen stored one bit, and there was a main memory of 32 x 32 dots, hence 1024 bits or 128 bytes of memory. The Williams-Kilburn tube's data can therefore be considered an early bitmap.

A bitmap – like Jacquard's punch cards, Bain's drum, the Bartlane tape or Baby's CRT memory – is an array of bits representing the brightness (and later the colour) of pixels of an image. The principle is nothing new: it can be seen in ancient Greek, Roman and Persian mosaics.

In 1957, US engineer Russell A. Kirsch scanned the brightness of an image at 30,000 points over a 2in square surface. The resulting 176 x 176 image of Kirsch's son was stored in the computer's acoustic delay line memory (see chapter 6) before being printed. As the first ever digital photograph to be printed, it can be seen today in the Portland Art Museum in Oregon.

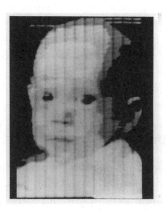

Figure 1.6: This digital image of Russell Kirsch's son, Walden, contained just 30,000 pixels.

Colouring in

Using a single bit for every pixel, we can store a pure black and white image, representing black with 0 and white with 1. However, figure 1.7 is a greyscale image, meaning it has several brightness levels, known as luminosities. If we increase the bit depth to two bits per pixel, we can store an image with four luminosities – for example, black (00), dark grey (01), light grey (10) and white (11).

We can extend this idea to give us colour. In 1972, the British engineer Michael Tompsett created the first digital camera image in genuine colour at Bell Labs in New Jersey, USA. Tompsett stored a picture of his wife using just eight bits per pixel, giving an image composed of 256 colours (2^8).[5]

> "Why would anyone want to look at their picture on a television set?" – Kodak's reaction when shown the first images taken with a portable digital camera invented by Steven Sasson, a Kodak engineer, in 1975.[6]

Microsoft created a standard bitmap format for Windows 3.1 with the file extension .bmp in 1994, but it doesn't compress well. In the late 1980s, the US internet service provider CompuServe (see chapter 9) created the more bandwidth-friendly Graphics Interchange Format (GIF) in 1989. With eight-bit colour, transparent backgrounds, good compression and support for simple animations, GIF – originally pronounced with a soft "g" like the peanut butter brand "Jif" – quickly became an internet standard and was supported by early browsers such as Netscape Navigator.

Meanwhile, the Joint Photographic Experts Group created the first JPEG standard in 1992, a bitmap format with 24 bits per pixel: eight bits each for red, green and blue luminosity. These values are calculated using a lossy compression algorithm called DCT, first proposed in 1972 by Nasir Ahmed, who was made an IEEE Fellow in 1985. The JPEG format is excellent for digital photography but does not support transparency, and with GIF's limitation of 256 colours, Portable Network Graphics (PNG) emerged as a rival format in 1996.

Long and winding paths

A Bitmap image is also called a raster, after the scanning process of a cathode ray tube. But dividing an image into square pixels each with a single value is not always the best way to turn visual information into numbers. Bitmaps do not scale well, causing blurring, or "pixelation", when enlarged. And when working with solid shapes, using square pixels to represent curves and diagonal lines is hardly ideal, causing serrated edges known as "jaggies". A solution was found that originated on radar screens.

Early radar operators viewed detected objects as dots or "blips" on a screen. As technology improved, these blips became shapes such as triangles, and the image could be annotated with codes, range lines and geographic features. Vector scanning is still used today in oscilloscopes and aircraft head-up displays and was also seen briefly in the 1980s arcade games *Asteroids, Star Wars* and *Battlezone*.

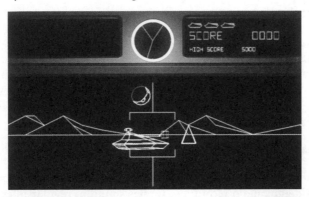

Figure 1.7: Atari's 1980 arcade game *Battlezone* featured vector-scanned white lines under a green and red overlay.

The vector-scanning method was the inspiration for vector image formats. Every shape is a line or polygon made by a set of x and y coordinates, or a curved path between two points defined by a mathematical function. This makes the image very precise and we can multiply the x and y values by a scale factor, enlarging an image while preserving quality. Defining shapes by perfect curves also ensures the image has no jagged edges. Of course, when rendered on a raster-scanned screen, even a vector image turns into square pixels, but at a high enough resolution the resulting edges still look smooth.

So, in the late 1990s, web users were looking for a vector file format. A small company called Adobe Systems had developed a vector-based file format for driving laser printers, called PostScript, back in 1984. Unfortunately, PostScript files don't scale well without becoming huge. The W3C sought an alternative and Scalable Vector Graphics (SVG) was chosen in 2001.

Pause here and consider Fertile Question 3: "JPG, GIF, SVG – why so many image file formats?"

_____

_____

Data about data

How does your browser know the dimensions of the image and the number of colours to use? The answer is metadata. The prefix "meta" comes from the Greek for "beside" or "beyond". In this case, we are going beyond the luminosity or path data to describe the nature of the data itself, such as the dimensions. Metadata can also include other information, and the JPEG standard includes camera model, f-stop and aperture in a section called "EXIF" data.

Sound ideas

Just as a bitmap records visual information as binary data by sampling squares of light, so a digital audio recording samples sound at regular intervals of time. The principle behind digital audio dates all the way back to 1937 when British telephone engineer Alec Reeves, of ITT's Paris headquarters, tried to solve the noise problem on long-distance telephone lines by sampling the sound into digital data and sending pulses over the line. Unfortunately, pulse code modulation (PCM) required expensive valve circuitry in the 1930s, and the idea was shelved until semiconductors made it viable 30 years later.

Digital audio players made their debut in 1982, with the launch of the compact disc (CD). A sample rate of 44.1kHz means that CD audio stores the amplitude of the sound wave as a single binary number 44,100 times every second. 16 bits allows more than 65,000 possible values per sample, and CDs have both left and right channels for stereo sound, providing a total of 16 x 2 x 44,100 = 1.4 million bits for every second of sound sampled.

This quantity of data (a three-minute pop song took up more than 30MB) was just too large for the internet in the 1990s, so compressed formats were invented, the most popular being MP3. Its lossy compression algorithm makes the file 75% smaller, and when affordable MP3 players emerged, digital music downloads boomed – bringing associated copyright controversies – in the late 1990s.

Microsoft preferred its own proprietary format, Windows Media Audio, and Apple's iTunes music store launched in 2003 with 200,000 songs encoded in the Advanced Audio Coding (AAC) format, considered superior to MP3. Many other formats sprang up, but the 1937 principle of pulse code modulation remained at the heart of them all. Just like text and images, strings of binary digits are given meaning by a code. By manipulating these binary digits, we can process real-world information.

What the hex?

Computer scientists work with binary data so often that they have devised an easier way of representing it, borrowed from maths. Binary is a base-2 system because it uses only two symbols, 0 and 1. This means that the place values of digits in a binary number go up in powers of two from right to left. Converting between binary and denary is fiddly because it involves repeated dividing or multiplying by powers of two. What if there was an easier way?

Enter the base-16 hexadecimal system, which takes its name from the Greek for six and 10. Hexadecimal uses the numbers 0-9 plus the letters A, B, C, D, E and F. With 16 different symbols available for every column, we can encode numbers from 0 to 255 using just two symbols every time. More importantly, each symbol correlates to exactly four bits. Long binary numbers can easily be converted to short, memorable strings of hexadecimal characters, and vice versa.

Colour codes in JPEG images and HTML pages can now be represented not with a string of separate decimal numbers like RGB (255, 192, 203) but as a single "hex" code: #ffc0cb, for example, which is the code for pink. The hash symbol denotes hex, just in case it's not obvious when there are no letters in the code, such as in the code for royal blue: #002366. The same number system is used wherever binary data needs to be made *human-readable*, including in assembly language programming, error codes and network addresses. It's important to remember, however, that the hex code exists only for human consumption. All data remains stored in binary: the only number system that can be processed by the computer. The byte 11010111 takes up the same amount of storage space whether we humans write it down in the original binary, or as the denary number 215 or the hex number D7.

Pause here and consider Fertile Question 4: "Why does a 700MB CD sound the same as a 50MB MP3 album?"

_____

_____

Codes for things

Because a computer is a general-purpose number-crunching machine, we can create an algorithm to process any information, as long as we find a way of expressing that information as numbers. In short, digitising analogue information makes it computable. Ada Lovelace would be pleased that her prediction turned out to be accurate: we did find a way to express all manner of objects by "the abstract science of operations".

TL;DR

At the heart of this topic is the idea that if we can turn information into binary data, we can use a computer to process it. Digital computers process binary numbers because they use two-state electrical signals. The challenge is therefore to find a transformation from real-world information to binary. This transformation is called encoding and it makes use of a code. ASCII and Unicode are used to encode text; JPEG, GIF, PNG do the same for bitmap images; and WAV, MP3 and AAC encode digital sound. But it's important to realise that there are virtually limitless ways of encoding information and these are just the techniques that are widely used, owing to their effectiveness or official recognition, or both.

Analogue-to-digital conversion is the process of mapping the original data to the digital representation, and it's vital to understand binary to really grasp the importance of bit depth, resolution and their effect on file size. Metadata is "data about data" and describes the contents of the file or something about the original information.

ACT ideas for the data topic

Now you've read the deep dive, let's do some serious learning activities to consolidate what you have read.

Question It – second attempt!

Answer these now that you have read the content.

1. Can a computer store and process anything we see or hear?
2. A Word document takes up just 100KB of storage until I insert images. Then it's 12MB – why?
3. JPG, GIF, SVG – why so many image file formats?
4. Why does a 700MB CD sound the same as a 50MB MP3 album?

Once you have made a strong attempt, go and read my suggested answers at httcs.online/learn-data. The questions are designed to provoke thought, and there is no exact right answer, but do you agree? Add something to improve your answer above before moving on.

ACT key skill: Cornell notes

This system for highly effective note-taking was developed at Cornell University, USA in the 1950s. You divide the page into sections (see figure 1.8). During a lesson or while watching a video, make notes on the right side. These can be short sentences, diagrams and tables, and if watching a video it's a good idea to grab screenshots[7] and annotate them. Immediately the lesson or video ends, make some notes in the "cues" column on the left. These can be keywords, key phrases or questions about the subject.

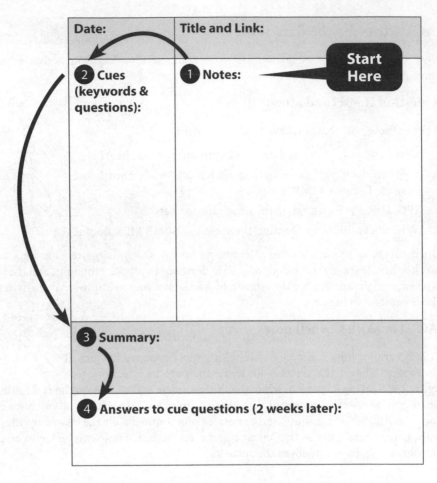

Figure 1.8: How to take Cornell Notes from a lesson or a video.

Then summarise the lesson at the bottom of the page in just a couple of sentences. Distilling a whole lesson like this is an example of transforming knowledge from one format to another, which makes you think hard about the topic. This is important because we remember what we think hard about. Memory is the residue of thought (psychologist Daniel Willingham again).

A few weeks later, go back to your page of notes and re-read it. Cover the notes column and read the cues column only. Can you define the keywords? What about the questions you set yourself, can you answer those? Did you miss a cue or is the summary a bit weak? Improve it now. Write another question for yourself, then come back later and answer it. Do this a few times and you should have mastered this lesson's topic.

☑ Make Cornell Notes now on "Representing Characters". Divide a sheet of A4 paper now like the image above ready for Cornell Notes (or open a word processor and make a table that looks like the image). Watch the seven minute video by Craig 'n' Dave™ at link.httcs.online/cndchars and make notes on your Cornell template. Save your notes somewhere safe and put a reminder in your diary to review them in two to three weeks' time. Rinse and repeat throughout the course! If you prefer digital notes, I recommend you keep them safe in OneNote, Google Keep or Evernote, but make sure any digital notes are backed up to the cloud.

ACT key skill: retrieval practice

Recalling key knowledge regularly makes it stick. One of my favourite ways is regular multiple-choice quizzing. A couple of summers ago I wrote 800 questions for Quizlet.com, available for free at link.httcs.online/quizletcs.

☑ Try one of the "data" quizzes now. Write a note in your diary to do it again in a few weeks. After doing the same quiz a few times you should be able to get 100% every time!

Stretch It

These activities will really stretch you.

Create your own character set

ASCII and Unicode are international standard character sets, but you can create your own character sets, optimised for different purposes.

☑ Try these "character set" tasks.

Create a character set for representing only English lower-case letters and five punctuation marks.

- How many bits are needed?
- What are the limitations of this character set?

☑ It would be possible to create a character set that encodes every word in the English language separately as a single number. Assuming there are 240,000 words in the Concise Oxford English Dictionary...

- How many bits would this require?
- Would this save space compared to ASCII?
- What advantages and disadvantages would this character set have?
- Explain why many bit patterns would almost never be used.
- If you created a character set of just emojis, how effective would this be as an international standard?

Make some notes here, then check my suggested solutions at httcs.online/learn-data. Remember, the object of the exercise is to think hard about the topic, because *memory is the residue of thought.*

_____

_____

_____

_____

_____

Relate It

These activities help you make sense of the theory.

Make your own image filter

Image filtering is performed by an algorithm. Think about what happens when you apply an effect such as "brighten". The numbers representing brightness have all been increased by a similar proportion. The "vignette" filter crops an image with an elliptical mask, dimming the edges of the picture as they approach the ellipse, finishing totally black.

☑ Consider these questions:

- What does a red filter do to the numbers in the image data?
- What algorithm is behind the vignette filter? (Hint: consider the distance of each pixel from the centre point and how you can use this to adjust the brightness).

☑ I've written some sample code on *replit.com* that uses Python with the PIL image library to create a red filter. Click here link.httcs.online/redfilter, "fork" and edit the code and make your own filters to change the colour cast of a JPEG image. If you want to make some more complex filters, computing teacher Martin O'Hanlon has created a whole course on using Python with image filters at link.httcs.online/fldatacourse.

_____

_____

_____

_____

_____

Link It

Link to programming
The image filter activity above shows how programming links to data representation. You could also see the links between programming and sound data, using a Python library such as wave (link.httcs.online/pymm).

☑ Try out this tutorial, which takes a look at learning how to use code to manipulate sound data: link.httcs.online/wavetut.

Link to architecture
Systems architecture can be linked to data representation in many ways. A Graphics Processing Unit (GPU) can improve the speed of image manipulation because its circuitry is designed to change hundreds of binary data values in the time the CPU takes to process just one.

☑ Watch this video (seven mins) and make Cornell notes to understand GPUs: link.httcs.online/gpus.

Link to memory and storage

Data relates closely to memory and storage, with more efficient representation methods requiring less storage capacity. Likewise, network bandwidth determines the size and quality of the images we can download, linking the topic to chapter 9.

☑ Watch "Crash Course Computer Science" video #23 for more information: link.httcs.online/crashgraphics.

Link to issues and impacts

☑ These are some of the impacts and issues of the Data topic. Have a think about how these issues affect you and your classmates now:

- Body image concerns caused by "photoshopped" images in the media (watch link.httcs.online/bodyimage).
- How the trend towards data-heavy multimedia websites widens the digital divide.
- The need for alt tags on images to improve accessibility.
- Problems with plagiarism and protecting copyright when images are used online.
- Bias in algorithms – how AI struggles to recognise non-white faces in images.

Links to other STEM subjects

The binary system pre-dates electronic computers by thousands of years. The I Ching, the ancient Chinese divination text that dates to at least 750 BC, contains 64 hexagrams each made up of six lines.

☑ Research the I Ching and explain how this is a binary code.

☑ Can you write a code to represent the 64 I Ching hexagrams with numbers?

☑ Write a program to input a hexagram as six strings (say "solid, broken, broken, solid, solid, solid") and return its name. Try to do this in as few lines as possible, perhaps storing a look-up table in a 2D array.

Like all number bases, binary is obviously a mathematical concept, so you could ask your maths teacher more about it or…

☑ Explore number bases here: link.httcs.online/funbases.

Quantity multipliers kilo, mega, giga and so on are common across all STEM subjects: think about kilometres, megawatts and gigahertz.

☑ Ask yourself: what has a gigabyte got in common with a gigawatt?

Link to geography

Before the 1961 ASCII standard, computers used different character sets, making communication difficult. ASCII was thus fundamental to the ARPANET project, which evolved into the modern internet (see chapter 9). The language of the web, HTML, is built on ASCII and its later replacement, Unicode. Without standard character sets we would not have the World Wide Web, with its profound effect on human communication.

☑ How important is a standard character set to global communications? How has this affected education, politics and economics?

Link to art and design

Digital images are important in art and design, and a digital photography club is a great place to really understand bitmaps, resolution, colour palettes and metadata. Likewise, the music department might already have digital music editing on the curriculum, and a digital music club could illuminate the topics of sound sampling, compression and plagiarism.

☑ Join a digital photography or digital music club, or start one if there isn't one available!

Unplug It

Paper bitmaps

Bitmap image creation is a great topic for unplugged activities.

☑ Print and solve the bitmap puzzles here: link.httcs.online/ pixelpuzzles.

See the links with the system software topic by reading the story of Susan Kare, who designed the first Mac icons (see chapter 8).

☑ Why not challenge yourself to design a 16 x 16 black and white icon? It's tough! Do it on graph paper like Susan did, or...

try pixel art online for free here: link.httcs.online/pixeleditor.

Build It

Micro:Bit LED bitmaps

The Micro:Bit has a built-in 5 x 5 grid of LEDs that can be set easily with blocks or text coding – perfect for learning about one-bit bitmaps.

☑ If you have a Raspberry Pi with the camera attachment, you can take pictures and process them with Python. You can use the Minecraft API to store these images in a "photobooth" within the Minecraft world.

Make a Minecraft Photo Booth on a Raspberry Pi with this tutorial: link. httcs.online/pibooth.

Sound engineering

Using the open-source software Audacity, you can get hands-on with sound recordings, finding out how the sample rate and bit depth affect sound quality and file size.

☑ Take this lesson on Oak National Academy and learn more about how digital sound works using free software "Audacity": link.httcs.online/oakaudacity.

Correct It

These are the common mistakes learners make when studying this topic, have you fallen into any of these traps?

Misconception	Reality
Binary can only represent numbers up to 255 in denary	Binary is the base-2 number system and like any number base it can represent any number. This misconception arises due to the lack of exposure to numbers larger than 255, numbers spanning many bytes. Remember, binary exists as a number base outside of the subject of computing, and it can represent numbers over 255 just like every other number base, you just keep adding digits or "places" on the left.
Binary place values start at 1 on the left and 128 on the right of an eight-bit number	Binary numbers are written right to left in order of rising place value, just like any other number base derived from the Arabic number system. The least significant bit, representing units, is always on the far right. Remember it's just a number base, like denary, so it follows all the rules of "place", with place values getting bigger from right to left.
The number of possible colours in a bitmap image is equal to the number of bits per pixel, so four bits gives four colours	The number of possible colours is calculated as 2bit depth, so four bits gives $2^4 = 16$ colours, and eight bits gives $2^8 = 256$ colours. Try out the unplugged bitmap activities mentioned above, with low bit depths from one to four, so you can see how the number of bit patterns, therefore the number of colours, doubles each time you add a bit.
Bit rate = sample rate	In digital audio, sample rate or sampling frequency is the number of times we sample an analogue signal in a given timeframe, usually measured in samples per second, or Hertz. Bit rate is the resulting quantity of bits in a given time frame, usually a second, calculated by this formula: bit rate = bit depth * sample rate. Bit depth is often called sample size, the number of bits per sample.
Encoding means using a secret code to keep data secure	A code is simply a means of transforming information into numerical data. ASCII is a code, as is the RGB colour code. The resulting number can be stored and processed by the computer. Codes are not ciphers – they are designed to be transparent and completely reversible. Ciphers are used to make information secret, which is the process of encryption, not encoding.

✅ Rank the misconceptions above in order of plausibility (which ones sound the most likely to be true!). For your top-placed misconception, make a presentation slide to explain the reality to a novice, to stop them falling into that trap.

Check It: Data representation

Concept	Need to learn 😞	Getting there 😐	Mastered 😊
I can explain why information is represented as numbers.			
I can state why computers use binary, relating binary to two-state electrical signals.			
I can define "number base", using the term "place value"			
I know what base-2 or binary numbers are and where they are used.			
I know what base-10, decimal or denary numbers are and where they are used.			
I know what base-16 or hexadecimal numbers are and where they are used.			
I can convert between number bases 2, 10 and 16 in all directions (six techniques).			
I can perform binary addition, including handling overflow.			
I can perform logical shifts on binary numbers and explain how they multiply or divide by two.			
I can define bits and bytes.			
I can explain the relationship between bits and quantity via powers of two.			
I can define binary file sizes bit, nibble, byte, kB, MB, GB, PB, TB and convert between units.			
I can define the term "character set" and explain why it is needed.			
I can describe ASCII, including its characteristics and limitations.			
I can explain the need for Unicode and describe its characteristics.			

Concept	Need to learn ☹	Getting there 😐	Mastered ☺
I can explain the relationship between number of bits and the available characters (via powers of 2) and calculate the number of bits needed to represent a given number of characters.			
I can explain characteristics of, and differences between bitmap (raster) & vector images,			
I can explain how a bitmap represents an image with reference to pixels and sampling.			
I can define pixels, bit depth (aka colour depth), dimensions and resolution of a bitmap image.			
I can explain the relationship between bit depth, resolution, dimensions and file size; performing calculations.			
I can define digital sound and explain the basics of analogue to digital conversion and sampling.			
I can define sample rate (aka sampling frequency), sample resolution (aka bit depth), duration of digital sound.			
I can explain the relationship between sample rate, sample resolution, duration and file size; and perform calculations.			
I can explain the need for compression and describe common techniques.			
I can define metadata and discuss its purpose and typical usage in text, image and sound files.			

✅ Complete the PLC mentioned at least monthly. For the topics you need to learn, make yourself a plan now. Rinse and repeat every month!

_____

_____

_____

_____

_____

_____

Endnotes

1   Charman-Anderson, S. (2021) "Ada Lovelace: Victorian computing visionary", Finding Ada, link.httcs.online/ada1

2   link.httcs.online/morse1

3   Updegrove, A. (2015) "The Unicode 8.0: a song of praise for unsung heroes", ConsortiumInfo.org, link.httcs.online/updegrove

4   link.httcs.online/bartlane

5   link.httcs.online/tompsett

6   Zhang, M. (2017) "What Kodak said about digital photography in 1 75", *PetaPixel*, link.httcs.online/kodakquote

7   To snip a portion of the screen, press Win-Shift-S on Windows, Comma nd-Shift-4 on a Mac or Shift-Ctrl-Show Windows on a Chromebook

CHAPTER 2. PROGRAMMING

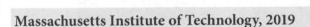

Massachusetts Institute of Technology, 2019

It's 10 April 2019. Late afternoon. The final stage of the pipeline of algorithms is executing. Dr Katie Bouman sits at her MacBook and watches as the picture of the black hole starts to appear. She and a team of computer scientists, astrophysicists and electrical engineers have been working on this project for three years. Five petabytes of data on half a tonne of hard drives from telescopes around the world arrived here at MIT more than a week ago, and the algorithms have been churning it ever since.

The M87 black hole appears tiny from earth – about as big as an orange would appear on the surface of the Moon. Refraction limits what we can see with our telescopes, so the very best image of the Moon from Earth consists of 13,000 pixels, but each pixel would then contain around 1.5 million oranges. To take an image of a black hole we would need an earth-sized telescope. We can't make one of those, but we can connect telescopes around the world, giving us lots of low-resolution images from different angles that could be processed by computers into a single image.

That's what Katie's team did, creating an Earth-sized computational telescope called the Event Horizon Telescope (EHT). Just as several different low-res images of the same face can be used to generate an accurate prediction of the real face, we can use these sparse, noisy images and put them together to create a more detailed picture. Katie has spent the last three years building a computational "pipeline" to do just that, feeding images from radio telescopes around the globe into the algorithm to eventually produce an image. The full story can be heard in Katie's TED talk[1], but what excites me is that the programming language chosen for all this computation is Python. At around 6.45pm on 10 April 2019, a researcher takes a picture of Bouman at her computer. We can see a code window on the right of her screen, which looks like the Matplotlib Python library. We can see the now famous image of the M87 black hole. But, most importantly of all, we are privileged to witness the joy of discovery. Katie presses her hands to her mouth, eyes full of wonder. An algorithm, her algorithm, has unlocked one of the secrets of the universe.

Figure 2.1: The moment of discovery: the world's first image of a black hole appears on Katie Bouman's laptop screen.

Code book

Katie Bouman knew, just like Ada Lovelace almost two centuries earlier, that programming could be fun and rewarding. In the monograph *The Art of Computer Programming*, the first volume of which was originally published in 1968, Donald Knuth writes:

"The process of preparing programs for a digital computer is especially attractive, not only because it can be economically and scientifically rewarding, but also because it can be an aesthetic experience much like composing poetry or music."[2]

Knuth's mammoth "programmer's bible" was included on American Scientist's list of "100 or so books that shaped a century of science", alongside *The Autobiography of Charles Darwin*, *A Brief History of Time* by Stephen Hawking and *In the Shadow of Man* by Jane Goodall. That a discipline only decades old shares such illustrious company says a lot about the importance of programming in our modern world.

Construction time again

Sequencing instructions is obvious – it's just one thing after another. But selection, iteration and subprograms are no accidents. The early assembly-language programmers had only a conditional jump instruction to play with, yet used this to build selection, iteration and subprograms because these constructs were so useful. In short, you learn how to code sequence, selection, iteration and subprograms not because they are imposed from above, but because they are natural features of algorithms!

One thing after another

Increasingly popular in universities throughout the 1970s, computer science was hardly taught at all in UK schools before 1982. A handful of pioneering maths teachers would have a Commodore PET or Apple II for a few high-flyers. The BBC's Computer Literacy Project, which ran from 1982 to 1989, changed all that. Schools received BBC Micros running BASIC with a tutorial and a selection of demonstration programs on cassette supported by a series of television programmes. A team at Acorn Computers in Cambridge, led by Steve Furber and Sophie Wilson[3], designed and built the machines.

My own high school had a single Commodore Pet when I arrived there in 1981. Only a few A-level students knew how to use it. By the time I embarked on Computer Studies O-level in September 1982, however, we had a 20 BBC Micros connected in a bus topology. A file server with twin 5¼-inch floppy disks gave us 200 MB of network-attached secondary storage on which to save our programs. (The BBC Micros had no secondary storage of their own back then).

BBC Basic included IF-THEN-ELSE and the much-despised GOTO statement (see chapter 4), but also features from structured programming including DEF PROC,

DEF FN, and REPEAT-UNTIL. Schools were encouraged to teach "computer studies" and the supporting TV series – The Computer Programme, broadcast in 1982 – explored the real-world applications of computers while teaching beginners how to code.

The first ever programming tutorial on UK TV was called "Just One Thing After Another" (the second episode in *The Computer Programme* series).[4] It demonstrated the sorting algorithms bubble sort and quick sort, and how to code a simple quiz using PRINT and INPUT. My teacher wheeled in a big-box TV and VCR every few weeks to show recordings of *The Computer Programme* and the BBC's follow-on series *Making the Most of The Micro* to my Computer Studies class.

The ICT years

The 1990s saw the rise of the PC (see chapter 6). By the turn of the century, digital literacy and application software skills were important for school-leavers. The UK government put information and communications technology (ICT) on the curriculum, but with no mention of programming, merely saying: "They develop, test and refine sequences of instructions as part of an ICT system to solve problems."[5]

The Royal Society's 2012 *Shut Down or Restart?* report suggested that programming go back on the curriculum: "Pupils should ... have the option to take further, topics such as: ... computer programming, data organisation and the design of computers; and the underlying principles of computing."[6]

The government responded and the 2014 UK national curriculum stated that computational thinking and programming should be taught in all schools. Programming was back on the syllabus!

It's not about code

Renowned Dutch computing pioneer Edsger Dijkstra said: "Computer science is no more about computers than astronomy is about telescopes." Programming is not about devices, or even keywords, punctuation and indentation; it's about problem-solving.[7]

When Peter Samson learned the opcodes of the TX-0, he did so to solve problems (see chapter 4). He wrote his music player to solve a problem, namely "How can I make this machine play Bach?" When Katie Bouman wanted to take a picture of a black hole by combining images from several telescopes, she wrote a program to solve that problem.

Programming exists to solve problems using a machine. First, we find a way to state the problem computationally, then we get a machine to perform the computation. The first part is what we now call computational thinking. It's easily the largest part of the process, but novice programmers often forget this, and sometimes expert instructors do too!

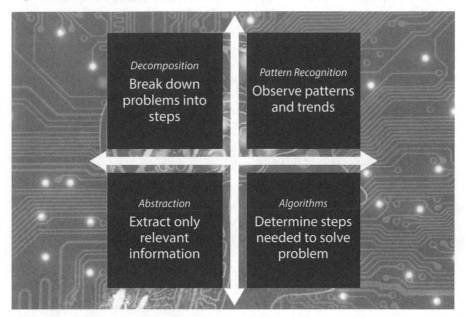

Figure 2.2: Computational thinking is the largest part of the programming process.

It's all about computational thinking

In 2017, Jeannette Wing, then head of computer science at Carnegie Mellon University in Pennsylvania, published a ground-breaking paper explaining that computational thinking (CT) is "formulating a problem in such a way that a computer can effectively carry it out."[8]

CT is not "thinking like a computer" but creating an algorithm to solve a problem with a computer. To better understand CT, watch the Oak National Academy lesson here: link.httcs.online/oakct. When devising a program, you use a set of skills collectively known as computational thinking: abstraction, decomposition, pattern-matching and algorithmic thinking. Only then are you ready to start writing down your algorithm…

No taxation without...

We need a clear, precise algorithm before we can code it. The same algorithm can be represented in many ways. You might find flowcharts easier than code, as they are visual and easy to construct. If we want to express an algorithm more accurately, we might use pseudocode: a precise written description of what a computer program or algorithm must do. Pseudocode should not have a formal syntax, but unfortunately you might see different pseudocode "syntaxes" in textbooks or practice exam papers. Don't worry about this too much, you can read and follow any style of pseudocode with a little practice, and exam boards generally accept any style of pseudocode or program code. Just make sure your algorithm is precise, unambiguous (has only one meaning) and solves the problem. Ask your teacher about this if you are unsure.

Concepts, not constructs

Unfortunately, most programming tutorials focus on syntax (the keywords, punctuation and order of statements in a program), not the process of *developing* a program to solve a problem. Stanford professor David Gries[9] explained in 1974 why this was a problem: "Suppose you attend a course in cabinet making. The instructor briefly shows you a saw, a plane, a hammer and a few other tools, letting you use each one for a few minutes. He next shows you a beautifully finished cabinet. Finally, he tells you to design and build your own cabinet and bring him the finished product in a few weeks. You would think he was crazy!"[10]

Most programming books are structured according to the language constructs – for example, the *while* loop and the *if* statement. These are the tools of code, but the process of choosing the right tools, using them in the right order, putting together the pieces, then testing and refining the product is more important. For this reason, one of my favourite websites for learning programming is *Runestone Academy*, where you can find this free Python course, organised by complexity of concepts, rather than syntax: link.httcs.online/runestone.

ACT ideas for programming

Developing CT skills through problem-solving

Computational thinking is a large part of programming, and you can develop CT skills without writing programs. The cs4fn.org, csunplugged.org and bebras.uk websites all offer fun challenges to stretch your CT skills. Try to identify the CT skills you are using and explicitly name and describe the algorithms you create when solving the puzzles. For example, in a CS4FN exercise such as "Searching to speak" (link.httcs.online/speak) make sure you identify the processes of decomposition, pattern-matching and evaluation. When you have a complete algorithm, write it down in a flowchart, pseudocode or natural English. Know that the process you have gone through is computational thinking and it is very important to programming.

Simon Johnson's *100 Ideas for Secondary Teachers: outstanding computing lessons* includes ten great computational thinking exercises, such as "Teaching with magic", "Human robot" and "Origami algorithms". Ask your teacher to get a copy and use it in lessons!

One algorithm, many representations

Each representation method (natural language, flowchart, pseudocode, program code) has strengths and weaknesses. Natural language is often easiest to express, so has a "low floor" (it's easiest to learn), while flowcharts help you to visualise the algorithm, so that loops and selection become obvious paths through the algorithm chosen by evaluating conditions.

Pseudocode can free you from worrying about syntax such as punctuation and how to indent, getting you close to the programmed solution. Practising different algorithm representations for the same algorithm can help you see and understand the concepts you need to learn: sequence, selection and iteration.

The notional machine

When Peter Samson wrote his music player program for the TX-0 in 1959 (see chapter 4), his "mind had merged into the environment of the computer".[11] To interpret, correct and write programs in a given language, we must construct in our heads a "notional machine", a basic understanding of what the system will do with your program. We need to be able to answer these questions, posed by researcher Juha Sorva:

> *"What can this programming system do for me? What are the things it can't or won't do? ... What changes in the system does each of my instructions bring about as my program runs? How do I reason about what my program does?"*[12]

Without a notional machine in your mind, you can't reliably predict what the computer will do with your code. This leads to misconceptions.

Misconception	Reality
Several lines of a program can be simultaneously active, especially a set of assignment statements	Programs are executed sequentially, top to bottom. Only one line of code is executed at a time, and it is not revisited (except through explicit control flow changes, such as loops or branches).
The computer can deduce the intention of the programmer from incomplete statements such as: `score + 1` `if age >= 18` `    "come in"` `    else "not allowed"`	Statements must be complete and syntactically correct, so the examples given (assuming Python is the teaching language) should be: `score = score + 1` `if age >= 18:` `    print("come in")` `else:` `    print("not allowed")`
Assignment statements, such as a = b, work in both directions, and either swap variables or make them always equal throughout the program execution	Assignment statements are made of two parts: the right-hand side of the assignment operator (=) is an expression that is evaluated, and the result stored in the variable on the left. Teaching this explicitly will prevent this misconception.
Meaningful variable names tell the computer what can be stored in them, so that, for example, smallest won't ever contain a value bigger than largest	Variable names are meaningless to the computer, so smallest can be given a value greater than largest.
IF statements are constantly active and will trigger whenever their condition is met	An IF statement is executed once; if the condition is true at the time of execution, the program branches. The statement then has no further effect on execution.
While loops terminate the instant the condition turns false, whatever statement causes this to happen	A while loop condition is evaluated on entry to the loop, and every time the code block inside the loop ends, not constantly during that code block execution.

✅ Try to construct a notional machine in your mind: picture the computer processing your statements and avoid the misconceptions mentioned. This will make your learning of programming more effective.

Exposure to many examples

Often you may not have seen a limited number of working examples of code before being asked to write your own. Some examples of misconceptions caused by limited exposure to variation are detailed here:

Misconception	Reality
Function arguments must be literals or constants (except where learners have seen special examples, such as the first line here) ``` r = int(input("radius?")) a = area(r) print(a) ```	The arguments of a function call can usually be any expression, including another function call. Therefore, this is valid for Python: ``` print(area(int(input("radius?")))) ```

Comparisons must appear within a conditional expression only. They cannot appear elsewhere – for example, in return or assignment statements
 	
``
if age < 18 or child == True:
  discount = True
else:
  discount = False
 	
if password == "summer" then:
  return True
else:
  return False
``
	Booleans are computable values just like numbers, so they can be used in expressions on the right-hand side of assignment statements and in return statements just the same.
	
	``
	discount = age < 18 or child
	``
	
	``
	return password == "summer"
	``

✅ Write a program in two lines of code that inputs the user's age, then outputs True if they are an adult or False if not. See httcs.online/learn-prog for a suggested Python solution.

Explicit live coding

Does your teacher do live coding? Researchers at the University of Wisconsin explained in 2018: *"In a live-coding session, the instructor thinks aloud while writing code and the students are able to understand the process of programming by observing the thought processes of the instructor".*[13]

✅ Watch a video of me live-coding a solution during remote teaching at httcs. online/prog, and fellow teacher Pete Dring has narrated a great many programs on his website here link.httcs.online/withcode.

Relate It

The building blocks of algorithms – sequence, selection, iteration and subprograms – can be learned with reference to other fields. For example, a recipe book, song lyrics and dance moves can be described algorithmically.

✅ Go cross-curricular and write an algorithm for composing a haiku or a limerick, or one for "parsing" a poem to see if it fits a certain lyrical form.

To make learning memorable, read stories! A rich source of stories that explain algorithm concepts can be found in Jeremy Kubica's books, beginning with Computational Fairy Tales,14 and you can find more on the Teaching London Computing website (teachinglondoncomputing.org).

Eliciting explanations

If you try to explain example code that someone else has written, or explain your own code, this helps you understand it.

✅ Try explaining sample code, in pairs or in small groups, or as part of a class discussion. Even explaining code to *yourself*, or to a plastic toy, aids understanding, which is why "rubber duck debugging" has made its way from the software industry into some classrooms! See link.httcs.online/duck for more.

Cheat sheets

When coding you should have a "cheat sheet" of syntax, or a link to a website where you can look it up, such as w3schools.com. We do not wish you to waste time and brainpower trying to remember the exact syntax of the while loop; it's far better that you think about the conditional expression that makes the loop perform properly and hence solves the problem.

Pair programming

Having one learner "drive" and another "navigate" is a way to share the cognitive load between two of you and add some fun to the process. This is practice is borrowed from the software industry's agile development approach.

✅ Pair up with another student, but don't forget to swap roles occasionally!

Chunking (aka subgoal labelling)

Chunking is breaking tasks down into simpler tasks, using the CT skill of *decomposition*. For example, if coding a quiz game, instead of simply trying to write the complete game, set yourself a subgoal such as "ask a single question and check the answer". The next subgoal might be "add a second question". The third could be "code a scoring mechanism", and the fourth could be "add a loop so the player gets three tries". Write a quiz game now, using these subgoals. Celebrate success at the completion of each subgoal!

Parsons problems

Writing a piece of code, breaking it into pieces and asking someone to reconstruct the program is known as making a *Parsons* problem. It tests your understanding of statements or constructs, and how they fit together, while removing any requirement to worry about syntax. An example can be seen in figure 2.3.

```
username = initial + last
```

```
first = input("firstname?")
last = input("lastname?")
```

```
print(username)
```

```
initial = first[0].upper()
```

Figure 2.3: A Parsons problem.

- ✅ Put the statements in the correct order to assemble a program that creates a username from the inputs of first and last names. There are lots of Parsons problems in the online programming courses at Runestone Academy (runestone.academy) and if you have a study partner you can make your own!

Block coding

Another way to release working memory for solid computational thinking is by going syntax-free altogether. Block-coding does this, in Scratch, Blockly, Alice, and App Lab. It's important that you use this opportunity to learn structured programming, however. Too many learners claim to "know Scratch", but a 2018 analysis discovered that three-quarters of all Scratch projects contained no selection or iteration, making them effectively just animations![15]

☑ A project by UK teenager Joshua Lowe, called EduBlocks, provides a drag-and-drop block-coding environment for Python, which can make it easier to transition from blocks to text: try it now at edublocks.org.

Physical computing

Physical computing – combining software and hardware to build interactive physical systems that sense and respond to the real world – can be more rewarding than just coding on a screen. But some products are easier to learn than others. The top five in order of complexity are the Makey Makey, Crumble, micro:bit, Arduino and Raspberry Pi.

☑ Ask your teacher if you can borrow one of these. A wealth of resources is available online including on raspberrypi.org and codeclub.org and makecode. microbit.org.

PRIMM

It might seem obvious but we didn't learn to write before we could read. For the same reason, we should read lots of working code before attempting to write it. Researchers at King's College London found success with a structure called PRIMM, which is now popular in schools.

Stage	Activities	Why
Predict	In pairs, look at a piece of code and ask students what they think it will do.	This activity encourages students to look for clues in the program that suggest what its function is.
Run	Run and check against your prediction. NB: have code in a shared area, don't make students waste time copying the code.	Opening prepared code moves the weight of ownership of any errors from the student to the teacher, increasing confidence and avoiding a challenging exercise to students who struggle with literacy at any level.
Investigate	There are lots of different activities you can do at this stage: trace the code, comment it, answer questions about it, label concepts, draw the flow of control, etc.	It takes many activities of this type, repeated in different forms in different lessons, for students to grasp the concepts in a secure way. We may think that writing one selection statement correctly means they have a good understanding of selection, but really "getting" this takes some time.

Stage	Activities	Why
Modify	Starting with working code, students are challenged to add modifications, beginning simply and increasing in difficulty.	The transfer of ownership moves from the code being "not mine" to "partly mine" as students gain confidence. This provides the scaffolding that students need to add small snippets of code and see their effect within a bigger program.
Make	Once confident, students can create their own program from scratch, like the example but their own design.	Design of a new program is an important skill and should start with planning and trying to construct a suitable algorithm. This is difficult, but gives students an opportunity to be creative and have the satisfaction of making their own program.

You can read more about PRIMM at link.httcs.online/primm. Your teacher might use it in the classroom, but even if they don't, you can improve your programming skill by following the PRIMM model anyway whenever you have a programming problem to solve, and there are lots of "PRIMM-able" problems on Pete Dring's website here link.httcs.online/withcode, where Pete's version of PRIMM is called KPRIDE. Meanwhile, Craig 'n' Dave call their programming course "TIME", but the principle remains the same.

The I in PRIMM

✅ During the "I" phase of PRIMM (or KPRIDE, or TIME), while investigating the code, try to ask questions about it to deepen your understanding, such as:

- What would happen if you swapped lines 2 and 3?
- What would happen if you gave it input of ___?
- What if you change the symbol on line 5 from > to < ?
- Line 5 shows a condition-controlled loop – why do we call it this?
- What will make the loop end?

Assessment

It's tempting to try a programming challenge and judge the final result but as a novice programmer you have a lot to learn, and each learning objective is a valuable step on the journey. So, we might check for understanding of key concepts on the way.

✅ You can test yourself using the free questions on Quizlet here: link.httcs. online/quizletcs.

TL;DR

Programming is not about code; it's about solving problems. The process of designing a program is the hard part, often called computational thinking, and developing CT skill is where we should spend our time. In all things we should consider cognitive load. We should make sure learners are thinking hard about what matters – getting better at designing programs using CT – and not about working out where the punctuation goes. Learning programming is a tough gig, but there is a wealth of resources at our disposal already – engaging with it should make you a more successful programmer.

Remember, you are engaged on a Grand Challenge. Programming is akin to learning a new language, yet typically you only get an hour a week in computing lessons, so becoming a programmer of any ability is an amazing achievement. Studying programming the right way can maximise your success and maybe you will go on to use computation to unlock yet more of the secrets of the universe!

Check It: Data representation

Concept	Need to learn 😣	Getting there 😐	Mastered 😊
I can read, write, analyse and refine programs written in a high-level programming language.			
I can write programs that make appropriate use of variables and constants.			
I can input and output data, and thus create programs that accept and respond appropriately to user input.			
I can use, understand and combine these statement types in programs: • variable declaration • constant declaration • assignment • iteration • selection • subroutine (procedure/function).			
I can write programs that use: • addition • subtraction • multiplication • real division • integer division • modulus (remainder).			
I can use boolean operators in programs: • NOT • AND • OR.			
I can use relational operators in programs: • equal to • not equal to • less than • greater than • less than or equal to • greater than or equal to.			

Concept	Need to learn 😞	Getting there 😐	Mastered 😊
I can describe the structured approach to programming and its advantages, including why we use subroutines.			
I can write programs that use built-in functions (e.g., int(), print()) and user-devised procedures and functions.			
I can call a random number generating function.			
I can write subroutines that use parameters to pass data within programs.			
I can write subroutines that return values to the calling routine.			
I know the difference between local and global variables and can explain why it is good practice to use local variables.			
I can use count-controlled iteration (e.g., the FOR loop) and condition-controlled iteration (e.g., WHILE)			
I can explain condition-controlled iteration with the condition at the start of the code block (WHILE) or the end of the code block (REPEAT UNTIL).			
I can manipulate strings in a program including: • length • position • substring • concatenation • convert character to character code • convert character code to character • string conversion operations.			
I can use array data structures (or equivalent e.g., lists) to solve simple problems.			
I can use record data structures (or equivalent) to solve simple problems.			
I can write programs with basic file handling operations: • open • read • write • close.			

Endnotes

1   Bouman, K. (2016) "How to take a picture of a black hole" (video), TEDxBeaconStreet, link.httcs.online/boumanted

2   Knuth,D. (1997) *The Art of Computer Programming, Volume 1: fundamental algorithms* (third edition), Addison-Wesley

3   Wilson was known at this time by her given name Roger and would transition from male to female taking the name Sophie in 1994

4   link.httcs.online/tcp

5   link.httcs.online/curric

6   Furber, S. (2012) *Shut Down or Restart? The way forward for computing in UK schools*, Royal Society, link.httcs.online/shutdown

7   link.httcs.online/dijkstrabio

8   Wing, J. M. (2017) "Computational thinking's influence on research and education for all", *Italian Journal of Educational Technology*, 25(2), 7-14, link.httcs.online/wing17

9   Gries was a professor at Stanford and Cornell universities and wrote *The Science of Programming* in 1981

10 Gries (1974) "What Should we Teach in an Introductory Programming Course?" in *Proceedings of the Fourth SIGCSE Technical Symposium on Computer Science Education*, New York, 81-89

11 Levy, S. (1984) *Hackers: heroes of the computer revolution*, Doubleday

12 Sorva, J. (2018) "Misconceptions and the beginner programmer" in Sentence, S., Barendsen, E. & Schulte, C. (eds) *Computer Science Education: perspectives on teaching and learning in school*, Bloomsbury

13 Raj, A. G. S., Patel, J. M., Halverson, R. & Rosenfeld Halverson, E. (2018) "Role of live-coding in learning introductory programming", *Proceedings of the 18th Koli Calling International Conference on Computing Education Research*, 1-8

14 Kubica, J. (2012) *Computational Fairy Tales*, CreateSpace

15 Grover, S. (ed.) (2020) *Computer Science in K-12: an A to Z handbook on teaching programming*, Edfinity

CHAPTER 3. ROBUST PROGRAMS

This topic explores how we make our programs robust, such that they don't fail or produce unexpected results.

Question It

First take a moment to contemplate these questions:

1. What proportion of a computing project should be testing?
2. Which is more effective: black-box or white-box testing? Why?
3. Can we make our programs foolproof?
4. What are all the ways in which computer systems can fail? Consider:

   a. Self-driving cars.

   b. The Mars rovers, such as Perseverance and Curiosity.

   c. A social media app.

Again, you will be prompted to think about these fertile questions at relevant points within the "Explore It" section, and you will get a second attempt at the end.

Explore It

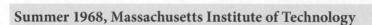

Summer 1968, Massachusetts Institute of Technology

Margaret Hamilton heads to MIT's Lincoln Laboratory to continue work on the flight software ultimately used for the Apollo space missions. This evening, as she often does because of scarce childcare, Hamilton brings her young daughter, Lauren, to work. While Lauren plays with the test rigs, Hamilton is programming. She and her colleagues are writing code for the Apollo Guidance Computer (AGC), inventing new ideas in computer programming as they go.

Lauren is "playing astronaut" with the test computer keyboard, hitting random keys until, to her delight, the simulation starts. But within minutes it has crashed: Lauren has selected a pre-launch program when she was already "in space", and the computer has wiped the navigation data. Hamilton is shocked, but is denied permission to alter the program to prevent this scenario from occurring on a real mission. When the "Lauren bug" happens for real during the Apollo 8 mission in December 1968, Hamilton is authorised to add validation code to prevent this type of crash in future.

20 July 1969, six miles above the moon

The Apollo 11 mission is 102 hours old. The launch site at Cape Canaveral, Florida, is a quarter of a million miles behind. Michael Collins remains in the command module, 20 miles above Neil Armstrong and Buzz Aldrin, who are descending to the lunar surface. Armstrong must control the braking thrust, avoid surface boulders and ensure a soft landing for the lunar module. But just seven minutes before touchdown, with fuel running low, an alarm sounds on the AGC. Four further alarms sound over the next few minutes, but Armstrong safely pilots the module past a boulder field. He declares, "Houston, Tranquillity base here. The Eagle has landed."

The software team at MIT can't relax – a malfunction during the return ascent to the command module could be catastrophic. The cause of the alarms must be located before the scheduled lift-off in 12 hours' time. Working through the night, they discover that the "rendezvous radar" was flooding the AGC with data, causing the computer to repeatedly restart. They realise the alarms are a feature, not a bug. The 1201 and 1202 alarms that sounded during descent were actually advice to the astronauts fired by Hamilton's recovery routine, named BAILOUT1, clearing an overloaded CPU and reloading only the top-priority programs, thus saving the mission.

Hamilton's innovations would later be described as "robust programming". Her work not only saved the first manned lunar mission, but launched a whole new discipline called "software engineering".

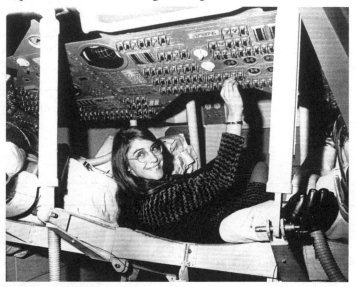

Figure 3.1: Margaret Hamilton pioneered the discipline of software engineering while working on the Apollo moon missions.

The software crisis

Computing power grew rapidly throughout the 1960s, as did demand for computer systems. Academic researchers, manufacturing, retail and finance were crying out for the new "ultimate labour-saving device", but with precious few programmers, the industry was in trouble. In 1968, at the first NATO Software Engineering Conference, Fritz Bauer, co-creator of the ALGOL language (see chapter 4), described the dire situation as a "software crisis". Programs were inefficient, buggy and late. Some companies collapsed due to failure of computing projects, all for want of good programmers.

Mother of invention

The crisis brought new languages such as Pascal and Ada, which encouraged structured programming. Whole new paradigms like functional programming appeared (see chapter 4). And crucially, program testing became a new discipline. Glenford Myers' 1979 book *The Art of Software Testing* defined it as the process of "finding errors". No longer was testing an attempt to declare a program bug-free.

Programmers were also encouraged to write quality code and make their programs foolproof – a technique we call "defensive design". Extensive test plans were now written during development, not after and, by the mid-1980s, formal software development methods with separate design, development and test phases were published.

> Pause here and consider Fertile Question 1: "What proportion of a computing project should be testing?"
>
> _____
>
> _____

Waterfall goes viral

The "waterfall" methodology split a software project into five key phases: requirements gathering, design, implementation, testing and maintenance.

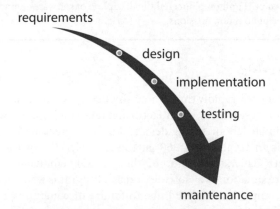

requirements

design

implementation

testing

maintenance

Figure 3.2: The waterfall method of software development was rigorous but inflexible.

The US Department of Defense formally adopted waterfall in 1988 whereupon it went viral. Dedicated testing teams would perform black-box testing, meaning they would treat the software as a black box into which they could not see. Testing would determine if the product behaved as expected: did it produce the expected output for a given input? This is distinct from white-box testing, a term later coined to describe testing with detailed knowledge of the code – a method known to early programmers simply as debugging.

> Pause here and consider Fertile Question 2: "Which is more effective: black-box or white-box testing? Why?"
>
> _____
>
> _____

More agility needed

By the 1990s, some companies were finding the waterfall methodology too cumbersome. Some projects had nothing to show for years of investment, due to rapidly changing customer requirements. Various new methods evolved, known collectively as agile methodologies. In agile, a project is broken into short bursts, delivering working software at the end of each burst. Agile can accommodate changing requirements more easily and it always delivers a working product.

Inevitable bugs

The cost of testing a complex program soon overshadowed its development costs, reaching on average 40% of total IT spend by 2018. In the critically acclaimed developer's manual *Code Complete*, Steve McConnell estimates that, in the average project, up to 500 errors are made in every 10,000 lines of delivered code. The Android operating system contains more than 10 million lines of code, while Windows has well over 50 million. Thus, our objective of robust programming is not to eliminate but to reduce the number of bugs, while making sure those that remain cannot cause catastrophe.

> Pause here and consider Fertile Question 3: "Can we make our programs foolproof?""
>
> _____
>
> _____

To illustrate the importance of robust programming, it's worth looking at some of the most high-profile software failures in history.

Software catastrophes

Therac-25 radiotherapy accidents

Between 1985 and 1987, the Canadian-built Therac-25 radiotherapy machine malfunctioned at least six times, giving patients massive overdoses of radiation. In the Therac-25, concurrent programming errors, also known as "race conditions", made it possible to select the wrong mode of radiation. If the operator typed "x" for X-ray treatment on the control terminal, then used the cursor-up key and corrected this to "e" for electron-beam therapy within eight seconds, the change would be ignored, leaving the machine set for a much stronger X-ray dose, while the electron-beam gun was in fact pointed at the patient. Three patients died and three experienced life-changing injuries.

Patriot missile rounding error

One of the most serious failures of robust programming resulted in the deaths of 28 American soldiers in the First Gulf War. An Iraqi Scud missile – usually an easy intercept for the Patriot missile defence system – evaded US defences owing to poor coding. The Patriot targeting computer attempted to calculate the time in tenths of a second by multiplying the system clock by 0.1. However, binary cannot exactly represent the decimal 0.1, so the computer makes an approximation, and the fewer bits you have to play with, the less accurate the approximation.

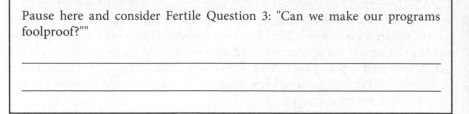 As an aside, you can try this yourself. In the Python Shell, or in any Python online IDE (Integrated Development Environment), just type 0.1 + 0.1 + 0.1 and see what happens.

```
Python 3.8.2 Shell                                    —   □   ×
File  Edit  Shell  Debug  Options  Window  Help
Python 3.8.2 (tags/v3.8.2:7b3ab59, Feb 25 2020, 23 ^
:03:10) [MSC v.1916 64 bit (AMD64)] on win32
Type "help", "copyright", "credits" or "license()"
for more information.
>>> 0.1 + 0.1 + 0.1
0.30000000000000004
>>>
```

Figure 3.3: Decimals must be approximated in binary, leading to rounding errors

The Patriot targeting computer used just 24 bits to represent 0.1, which meant every calculation was out by 0.000000095 seconds. These errors were cumulative, so after 100 hours of uptime the targeting clock was out by a third of a second. That might not seem a lot, but a Scud missile can travel 600 metres in that time, so when the targeting computer saw empty sky where a missile should be, it failed to launch, and 28 souls perished in February 1991.

What could go wrong?

The average small-to-medium business now stores around 48 TB of data. Algorithms churn this data, making decisions that are important to their customers, including credit checks, medical supply orders and insurance claims. If the data is inaccurate, customer service is affected, people may be disappointed or even harmed, and the reputational damage can be enormous. Keeping your data accurate and consistent is called data integrity; it's achieved via sanitisation, authentication and validation.

Validation means checking that the input is reasonable, not that it's correct: we can't know a user's age, but they can't be more than 150 years old. Validating inputs can prevent "downstream" errors that could be catastrophic, such as charging someone 100 years' worth of interest or prescribing the wrong medicine.

Authentication means verifying someone's identity before granting access to your system, and access controls ensure they have the correct authority before allowing data to be accessed or changed. For example, counter staff in a bank might be able to raise transactions of up to £10,000 but be prevented from moving higher amounts.

Implementing sanitisation, validation, authentication and access control is often described as "anticipating misuse". This is a key feature of defensive design – writing programs that won't fail despite user error or malicious intent.

Pause here and consider Fertile Question 4: "What are all the ways in which computer systems can fail?"

_____

_____

Move fast and break things

While the story of computing is sometimes called the "third industrial revolution" (after steam-powered machines and the invention of the production line), it's also the history of spectacular mistakes. Some were down to poor program design or inadequate testing; most were driven by a desire to deliver the product quickly and cheaply. Over time, however, the computing industry has learned at great cost the value of building robust systems through defensive design techniques and rigorous testing. Margaret Hamilton's BAILOUT1 routine, which saved the Apollo 11 mission, remains a lesson from history that resonates today.

TL;DR

Early programmers designed and debugged their own programs. Building in code to prevent failures due to user error or hardware failure was pioneered by Margaret Hamilton for the Apollo space programme. Her work led to the creation of a new discipline: software engineering, popularised by a NATO conference in 1968. New techniques and tools were created throughout the 1970s to address the "software crisis" and improve software quality, including new languages that encouraged structured programming, and new paradigms such as functional programming.

Testing began to be recognised as separate from debugging in the 1970s, with Glenford Myers publishing *The Art of Software Testing* in 1979. The software development life cycle (SDLC) was formalised in the 1980s and the waterfall model became commonplace after the US Department of Defense adopted it in 1988. The waterfall model described several distinct project phases: requirements gathering, design, implementation, testing and maintenance. Software testing became a separate discipline performed by a different team to the developers.

Industry found the waterfall model unresponsive to changing user requirements, and iterative techniques, often known as "agile", grew popular in the 1990s. Many companies began to employ test automation software as testing consumed a larger part of the IT budget.

Modern robust programming includes anticipating misuse through authentication, sanitisation and validation, plus a formal development methodology such as agile, structured programming techniques focused on modular, maintainable code, and a rigorous testing regime.

ACT ideas for robust programs

Now you've read the deep dive, let's do some serious learning activities to consolidate what you have read.

Question It – second attempt!

1. What proportion of a computing project should be testing?
2. Which is more effective: black-box or white-box testing? Why?
3. Can we make our programs foolproof?
4. What are all the ways in which computer systems can fail? Consider:

    a. Self-driving cars.

    b. The Mars rovers, such as Perseverance and Curiosity.

    c. A social media app.

As in chapter 1, once you have made a strong attempt, go and read my suggested answers online at httcs.online/learn-robust. Do you agree with my suggested answers? If not, why not?

ACT key skill: sketch notes and mind maps

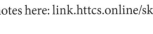

Diagrams are valuable learning tools. Making a diagram helps us understand and remember a topic. Sketchnoting is a technique for making visual notes invented by designer Mike Rohde in 2006, and you can read about it here link.httcs.online/sketchnoting. Computer science teacher Alan O'Donohoe recommends sketchnoting for users of his online course or "MOOC" and you can see some of his students' sketchnotes here: link.httcs.online/sketchnotes.

☑ Make a sketchnote on a lesson you just had today or on a Craig'n'Dave video.

Stretch It

Why did it fail?
Re-read the software error stories from this chapter and discuss with your classmates what might have gone wrong.

☑ Think about the stages of software development: design, coding, testing. Where did the error creep in? If you had been in charge of the software, what would you have done differently to prevent the failures?

Was Dijkstra right?
Discuss with a partner Dijkstra's statement that we "should not introduce the bugs to start with". Think about how this can be achieved. Is the choice of programming language and paradigm important? What about separating programming from testing?

Peer testing
☑ In pairs, code a program and write a test plan for it, then swap seats and test your partner's program. Is this more effective than testing your own program? Try this again, but deliberately introduce errors into the program before giving it to your partner for testing to see if the tester finds them!

Robotic verification, yes or no?
☑ Get your teacher or a study partner to specify (that means make a design for) an algorithm in a flowchart or pseudocode, then you write some code for it. Without running the code, check it against the specification to prove that the program will work. Do you think this can be automated, and how? If not, why not?

Validate everything?
Re-read the "Lauren bug" at the start of this chapter. NASA was reluctant to allow Margaret Hamilton to add the code to prevent this bug, claiming that no highly trained astronaut would make that mistake. Of course, Jim Lovell went on to press the wrong key on the Apollo 8 mission.

☑ Should we validate every input, even those we are not expecting?

Link It

Link to architecture
Computer systems are made of hardware and software. We learn in the architecture topic that hardware has a limited reliable life and it eventually breaks down. When we move controls from hardware to software, as in the design of the Therac-25, we overcome potential hardware issues, but at what cost?

✅ Think: would you prefer a manual dial or a computer program to control your radiotherapy dose, and why? What would make you trust the software?

Link to languages
High-level code was designed to help programmers create complex code more easily. But we learn in the languages topic that low-level code is often used for mission-critical programs because it can be made more robust. Why is this?

Link to issues and impacts
✅ What are the ethical issues of poor-quality software? Clearly it can kill, but what is the impact of poor-quality code on the end user of the following products:

- Medical equipment
- Computer games
- A shopping website
- A social media app
- A bank

Industry experts suggest that 25-40% of a project should be spent on testing. Is this reasonable? What kind of projects can get away with less than this? What would require more?

Translation programs are now widely used to help everyone from travellers to researchers understand text in a foreign language.

✅ What would be the impact of translation errors in:

- A piece of school homework
- An official document such as a trade agreement
- An instruction document for a piece of medical hardware (like a radiotherapy machine)

Link to design and technology

☑ Recall the design process that you meet in design and technology. How does "iterative design" relate to software development?

Link to science

Some branches of science rely heavily on computer models. These can be enormously complex – for example, a weather model or a model of particles in a nuclear reactor. How can we ensure these are robust?

Relate It

Vending machine woes

Consider a vending machine that dispenses drinks and snacks.
Think of all the ways that the system could fail, and how we could design it defensively to mitigate failures. Maybe create a table listing possible failures and their mitigations:

Failure	Mitigation
Mechanical failure while vending	Sensors recognise the failure and refund the money.
Customer walks away mid-vend	Machine times out and resets for the next customer after two minutes of inactivity.
Insufficient coins in the machine to give accurate change	Warns customer that no change is available before vending, and ensures they are OK with this.
Power failure while vending	Sets a non-volatile flag when beginning to vend. Saves the values of credit and choice of product in non-volatile storage. On power-up, checks the state of this register and resumes vend if flag set.

☑ Can you add more rows to this table?

☑ Choose another embedded system, perhaps a ticket barrier or a lift in a tall building, and write a similar table for it.

Impenetrable code

Get your teacher to show you some code that is poorly written, without meaningful variable names, indentation or comments.

☑ Try to explain what the code does. When you have attempted this, why not rewrite the code in a maintainable way and ask someone else to explain it. What does this tell you about the importance of maintainable code?

Craig 'n' Dave provide such an activity in their premium resources.

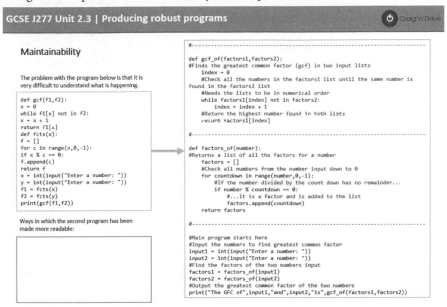

Figure 3.4: An exercise in code maintainability from the Craig 'n' Dave premium resources.

Unplug It

Computer programs can be debugged and "tested" through a "dry run" walkthrough: the programmer or tester looks over the code and determines what will happen at each line. Sometimes they will use a trace table to keep track of the contents of variables. Performing walkthroughs of algorithms while unplugged helps you develop your understanding of the code, and builds a mental model called the "notional machine" (see chapter 2).

Build It

Using the Raspberry Pi, micro:bit or similar, you can develop products that use physical devices. Many projects can be found at projects.raspberrypi.org. Testing is a vital part of any project, so make sure you spend plenty of time doing it!

Apply It

Robust design and effective testing should be part of all the project work that you undertake. Iterative testing and final testing should be built into any projects you do, especially large "makes" and programming problems.

Correct It

Misconception	Reality
Validation is "checking the input is correct"	Validation is "checking the input is reasonable". Learners confuse validation with verification, sanitisation and authentication. These processes must be clearly explained and contrasted.
We only need to test the code we have changed	When adding or changing code, learners will often test the new section of code, without considering the rest of the program. Testing the unchanged code to ensure that its behaviour has not changed is called regression testing and it should be encouraged.
We test for expected results only. **For example, after writing this code to test for vowels** `l = input("letter?")` `if l in "aeiou":` ` print("vowel")` `else:` ` print("consonant")` **novices may test with single vowels only, or single lowercase letters only, or single mixed-case letters only**	Testing should cover a sample of all possible input values including normal, boundary and erroneous data (also known as valid, extreme or invalid). Learners often assume that the point of testing is to check that the program performs as expected when expected data is entered. They often don't consider the possibility of erroneous data being entered – for example, letters in the wrong case, input having the wrong data type or a value out of range.
Black-box testing is performed by hackers: confusion with black-hat hacking	Black-box and white-box testing are often confused with black-hat and white-hat hacking, with students believing that black-box testers are malicious. In fact, black-box testing simply means treating the program as a black box into which we cannot see, therefore we check outputs against those expected for given inputs.

Misconception	Reality
Debugging and testing are only necessary because we are novice programmers	Learners often assume that they need to debug and test their code because they are novices, and when they become more experienced they will write flawless code first time. It's important to stress that debugging and testing is a vital part of developing new programs, and experienced programmers do a lot of it! The teacher live-coding in front of the class, then debugging and testing, is very valuable here.

Check It: Robust programs

Concept	Need to learn 😞	Getting there 😐	Mastered 😊
I can define defensive design and state why it is necessary.			
I can explain "anticipating misuse" and give an example.			
I can define "authentication" and give an example.			
I can describe input validation and give examples in code or pseudocode of range check, lookup check, type check and presence check.			
I can explain input sanitisation and why it is needed to defend against SQL injection.			
I can say why maintainability of programs is important, and give examples of maintainability using subprograms, naming conventions, indentation, whitespace and comments.			
I can identify syntax and logic errors and explain the difference.			
I can refine algorithms (e.g. to improve performance or correct logic errors).			
I can explain the purpose of testing.			
I can select and use suitable test data that is normal. boundary, invalid or erroneous.			
I can describe types of testing: black-box and white-box.			
I can explain the phases of testing: iterative and terminal/final.			

CHAPTER 4. LANGUAGES AND TRANSLATORS

This topic covers how we get programs into a computer and how those programs are turned into instructions for the CPU.

Question It

Take a moment to contemplate these questions:

1. If we can code in assembly language, with instructions like INP, STA and ADD, why do we need high-level languages?
2. Why are there so many programming languages?
3. Why do video games have a format, such as PC, Xbox, PlayStation?
4. Why did Java become so popular?
5. Can a spreadsheet full of formulas be considered a computer program?
6. Why do interpreted languages run slower than compiled languages, and why does this matter less today?

Again, you will be prompted to think about these fertile questions at relevant points within the deep dive, and you will get a second attempt at the end of the section.

Explore It

Massachusetts Institute of Technology, 1959

A computer is playing Bach. The programmer, Peter Samson (he likes to be called a hacker), is pleased with the result and is now working on a general-purpose music decoder that will read in codes from paper tape and play the corresponding notes on the computer's speaker. These are ground-breaking programs: the first use of a musical code to produce sounds in real-time, bringing to life Ada Lovelace's idea from 1843 (see chapter 1). But how did we get here?

The story starts in the spring of 1959, when MIT offers a new course called programming taught by John McCarthy. McCarthy has recently established a controversial new field of study, naming it artificial intelligence, and caused a stir by programming MIT's million-dollar IBM 704 mainframe to play chess.

With around 18 kilobytes of RAM and able to perform 12,000 calculations per second, the valve-built 704 is impressive but working with it is frustrating. Programs are loaded from punched cards and processed in batch from start to finish. Output appears on the printer if all goes well, while any bugs require the programmer to start all over again. This "batch processing" concept makes working on the 704 slow and tedious. But things are about to change.

MIT's military research department, known as the Lincoln Lab, has donated its $3 million TX-0 to McCarthy's faculty. The "Tixo" has less memory than the 704 but several huge advantages: transistors, a display, a speaker, and a new typewriter-like input device called a Flexowriter. Thanks to its silicon innards, the new machine can execute 100,000 calculations per second. Most importantly to Samson, a hacker can sit at the terminal and see and hear the effects of their program – and even modify it while sitting there.

The speaker is designed not as an output device, but to assist the operator. It simply clicks to indicate the contents of the 14th bit of the accumulator (see chapter 5), so if it stops clicking, that means the program has finished or, if you're unlucky, entered an infinite loop. But Samson sees a way to exploit this feature to make music. A simple program feeding the accumulator with the right sequence of data will cause the speaker bit to turn on and off at the correct frequency to play a note, albeit a simple, square-waved note. Push lots of these numbers into the register in the right sequence and you have a tune. Samson teaches the Tixo to play classical music in just 4K of memory, and the hackers of MIT are impressed.

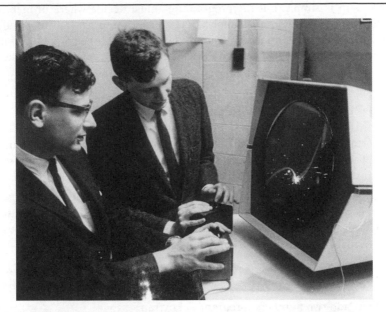

Figure 4.1: Peter Samson and Dan Edwards in 1962 playing Spacewar!, often considered the first computer game.

Assembly line

Samson wrote his music player in assembly code, using short keywords called mnemonics, each one consisting of an opcode and an operand. Every CPU has a finite instruction set of opcodes that it can process. Each assembly code instruction represents exactly one machine code instruction. A simple program called an assembler turns the code into binary using this one-to-one mapping.

A small program to add two numbers using the LMC Instruction Set (see chapter 5) might look like this:

```
INP     # input number into accumulator
STA 99  # store contents in RAM location 99
INP     # input number into accumulator
ADD 99  # add contents of RAM location 99
OUT     # output contents of accumulator
```

This program is simple, but the programmer must decide where in memory to store the data. Anything more complex, like a program to play a tune, would run to hundreds of lines and require a good understanding of the computer's internal workings: its registers, buses and memory. As Steven Levy explains in Hackers:

"When you programmed a computer you had to be aware of where the thousands of bits of information were going from one instruction to the next, it was almost as if your mind had merged into the environment of the computer."[1]

Clearly, this hacker-level immersion in the bits and bytes of a computer is beyond most mortals, but fortunately abstraction has an answer. To add two numbers, instead of writing INP, STA 99, INP, ADD 99, OUT, what if we could just write English instructions and let the computer decide what binary codes are required?

One floor below the Tixo, McCarthy is doing just that on the 704. His chess program is coming along nicely in a mixture of assembly code and Fortran. This early high-level language was developed by a team at IBM, led by John Backus, with the aim of making mathematical computation easier.

Coding in English

Here's that "add two numbers" program in Fortran:

```
read *, a, b
s = a + b
print *, s
```

This should look familiar if you've seen Python or JavaScript. But, as we'll see in chapter 6, the computer doesn't understand anything; it can't read this code, much less comprehend it, so how can we run this program? The answer is translation. The high-level source code passes through a translator program called a compiler, which generates the binary machine code, also known as object code.

Fortran was not the first high-level language, but it was the first commercial success. The 1960s saw an explosion of high-level languages including ALGOL, COBOL and LISP.

ALGOL, short for algorithmic language, was designed between 1958 and 1968 by a committee including Backus and McCarthy, plus other giants of computer science mentioned in this book, including Peter Naur, Fritz Bauer and Alan Perlis. In addition, many variants of ALGOL were created, including versions by Edsger Dijkstra and Niklaus Wirth.

ALGOL was designed from the beginning to promote structured programming; it was the first high-level language to include code blocks delimited by BEGIN and END, selection with IF-THEN-ELSE, conditional iteration with WHILE and control structures for procedures. These features made their way into all subsequent imperative languages including JavaScript and Python.

> Pause here and consider Fertile Question 1: "If we can code in assembly language, with instructions like INP, STA and ADD, why do we need high-level languages?"
>
> _____
>
> _____

Structured code – it's the future!

The standard control structures pioneered in ALGOL should be familiar to us today. We use them for program flow control using sequence, selection, iteration and subroutines. A programmer in an ALGOL-like procedural language, such as C or Python, can easily pick up how to code in another, such as Ruby or C#, because the basic structure of the language – the building blocks with which programs are constructed – remains the same. Only the syntax changes.

Syntax is the grammar of a language. It defines what is legal code: the keywords, punctuation and structure of programs. Code can have correct syntax, but still not compile or run correctly if it contains semantic or logic errors.

Wordy number cruncher

In parallel to academic strands of language development was the business-oriented field. In 1959, the computer scientist and naval officer Grace Hopper created the Common Business-Oriented Language, or COBOL.

```
IDENTIFICATION DIVISION.
PROGRAM-ID. hello.
PROCEDURE DIVISION.
DISPLAY "Hello World!".
STOP RUN.
```

The ubiquitous "Hello World" program in COBOL.

COBOL was a notoriously wordy language, designed for batch processing of financial data for tasks like billing or insurance quotes. But it was easy to learn and had powerful input/output capabilities. COBOL compilers were written for all the major mainframes of the day, including IBM, Burroughs, UNIVAC and Honeywell. COBOL was to dominate the business software market for more than three decades, and code written in COBOL still runs on many finance and utility company mainframes today.

More importantly, Hopper did the heavy lifting in the field of compiler design, giving us the many stages of compilation: lexical analysis, syntax analysis, code generation and linking.[2]

The academic's choice

```
begin
    if a>=b then
        max := a
    else
        max := b
end;
```

A fragment of code in Pascal (1970) to find the higher of two numbers. This syntax should look familiar to Python programmers.

ALGOL committee member Niklaus Wirth forked the ALGOL language (made a new version of it) and added new features like linked lists, graphs and trees. He released this as Pascal in 1970. The language was popular in education and the mini-computer software market throughout the 1970s until overtaken by C and VB.

Military precision

By 1975, the number of programming languages in use in embedded systems worried the US Department of Defense enough that it formed a working group to find a new all-purpose language. The ambitious project resulted in the creation of Ada, first released in 1980 and still in use today in transport systems, military hardware and space technology, but is rarely used commercially.

BASIC instinct

Beginners' All-Purpose Symbolic Instruction Code (BASIC) was first developed in 1964 by John Kemeny and Thomas Kurtz at Dartmouth College in New Hampshire, US, to allow students to write code for mathematics. Versions were produced for the new mini- and micro-computers that sprung up throughout the 1970s, with Bill Gates's version for the hobbyist's Altair computer at the centre of the first big software piracy dispute.[3]

The BBC's Computer Literacy Project, which ran from 1982 to 1989 (see chapter 2), was centred around BBC Basic running on a machine designed by Acorn Computers in Cambridge, UK. BASIC influenced the design of Microsoft's Visual Basic, which was widely used to build Windows applications in the 1990s; a version called VBA is still bundled with Office for writing macros.

C for miles

Dennis Ritchie wanted to create utilities for the Unix operating system he had created with Ken Thompson (see chapter 8) so he took and simplified BCPL from the University of Cambridge, UK. He called his simplified version "B", but it was slow and limited, so Ritchie upgraded it and "C" was born.

C provides structured programming features borrowed from ALGOL, but is a hackers' programming language providing low-level access to memory. This makes C powerful, but also dangerous: buggy or malicious code can have disastrous effects if the wrong portion of memory is altered. More forgiving languages like Python manage memory on behalf of the programmer. Descendants of C include object-oriented versions Objective-C and C++, and a proprietary Microsoft version called C# designed for use on the web and mobile platforms.

Pause here and consider Fertile Question 2: "Why are there so many programming languages?"

_____

_____

Cookie-cutter coding

In 1962, the Norwegian developers Ole-Johan Dahl and Kristen Nygaard created Simula, a programming language developed from ALGOL 60 to simulate integrated circuit designs. The 1967 version, Simula 67, was the world's first object-oriented language, sporting classes and objects.

A class is like a blueprint, sometimes called a "cookie-cutter" for objects. The object behaves according to its class's attributes and methods. A programmer simply defines all the classes of object and how they behave, rather than writing long chains of instructions. Object-oriented programming is well-suited to games development, simulation and neural networks.

Pure class

Player
name: string score: integer
get_name() get_score() set_score(new_score)

```
class Player
    private name
    private score
    public procedure new(given_name)
        name = given_name
        score = 0
    endprocedure

    public function get_name()
        return name
    endfunction

    public function get_score()
        return score
    endfunction

    public procedure set_score(new_score)
        score = new_score
    endprocedure
endclass
```

Inspired by Simula, a team funded by the Advanced Research Projects Agency (ARPA) at Xerox PARC created Smalltalk, a highly influential early OOP language. The team, led by Alan Kay and Adele Goldberg also broke new ground in "human-computer symbiosis", with interactive time-shared computers, graphics screens with overlapping windows and a pointing device we would recognise as a mouse. The influence of Smalltalk can be seen in modern OOP languages including C++, C#, Java and Python (yes, Python can be used as a simple procedural language, but it also supports OOP!). Above is an example of a class definition, shown both in Unified Modelling Language (UML) and in the OCR Exam Reference Language (formerly known as pseudocode). This class could be used to define player objects in a game.[4]

Well, I declare!

ALGOL was an imperative language in which we write instructions for the computer to perform, like Fortran, ALGOL, Pascal, C++, Python and JavaScript. LISP belongs to a different paradigm called functional programming. A subset of declarative programming, a functional program describes functions that evaluate expressions.

Functional languages include LISP, Erlang, Clojure, Scheme and Haskell. They have no variables, only identifiers for values contained within expressions. Haskell is used widely in academia, but also for analysing financial risk at the Dutch bank ABN AMRO and transforming digital music into musical notation in the Chordify app.

```
fac :: (Integral a) => a -> a
fac 0 = 1
fac n = n * fac (n - 1)
```

A Haskell program to calculate factorial.

Functional programming avoids side-effects. Each function always returns the same value for the same parameters passed to it, and nothing else changes. This makes behaviour highly predictable and less prone to error. Because functions are so versatile, there is always an elegant way to get the job done, meaning functional programs tend to be shorter, with the solution much closer to the problem (see above).

Pause here and consider Fertile Question 3: "Can a spreadsheet full of formulas be considered a computer program?"

_____

_____

Prolog

```
likes(ryan, cheese).
likes(ryan, wine).
not(likes(lila, wine)).
likes(inez, wine).
likes(inez, X) :- likes(X, wine).

?- likes(ryan, wine).
 yes.
?- likes(inez, ryan).
 yes.
?- likes(inez, lila).
 no.
```

A Prolog program is a set of predicates and queries.

In another family of declarative languages, we simply make statements about relationships between objects. In 1972, Alain Colmerauer and Philippe Roussel at Aix-Marseille University in France wanted to formally describe the French language. With help from Robert Kowalski of the University of Edinburgh they created the first logic programming language, Prolog.

In a logic language we write statements to describe facts about the world. Querying these facts produces useful output (see above). The language is good for AI applications such as voice response or expert systems.

Code once, run anywhere

Back in the imperative world, and before 1995, you would need multiple compilers for multiple devices, creating separate object code "executables" for each machine. This is because each machine had its own low-level instruction set. Java turned this concept upside down. Initially planned for the digital cable television industry, Java was perfect for the growing web application market in the late 1990s.

> Pause here and consider Fertile Question 4: "Why do video games have a format, such as PC, Xbox, PlayStation?"
>
> _____
>
> _____

Named for designer James Gosling's favourite coffee bean, Java is compiled only once, to an intermediate "bytecode". This portable bytecode is then interpreted directly on the platform, by a Java virtual machine (JVM). The code itself is written just once, and compiled just once, but is runnable anywhere with the right JVM. This gave Java a portability advantage and it quickly became the language of choice for web apps, and later smartphone apps.

> Pause here and consider Fertile Question 5: "Why did Java become so popular?"
>
> _____
>
> _____

The web goes interactive

Not to be confused with Java, JavaScript was developed to add interactive elements to Netscape Navigator, the most popular browser on the World Wide Web in the late 1990s. Originally called LiveScript, the name was changed shortly after release, possibly to jump on the Java bandwagon, and the similar names have been causing confusion ever since. JavaScript is supported by all major web browsers, but it's also a programming language in its own right. It's used in web and mobile apps, and as a teaching language.

Perl's a winner

JavaScript is the language of choice for the browser-side code. Meanwhile Perl is popular on the server-side. Server-side code is executed on the web server to serve up dynamic web pages, for example, when retrieving data from a database. Python creator Guido van Rossum loved Perl and once admitted that if it had been available on his system at the time, he would never have created Python!

Joyful coding

The Zen of Python is a collection of guiding 19 principles published on the Python mailing list in 1999 by major Python contributor Tim Peters. It includes these principles:

1. Beautiful is better than ugly.
2. Explicit is better than implicit.
3. Simple is better than complex.
4. Readability counts.
5. There should be one – and preferably only one – obvious way to do it.

Van Rossum launched Python in 1991 (he was a big fan of the British sketch show Monty Python's Flying Circus). He wanted his new language to be fun, simple and highly extensible. Extensibility means anyone can write code libraries to add features to the language. For simplicity, Python has very little punctuation compared with C++, Java and JavaScript. Python forces readability by using indentation to show where code blocks begin and end. Gone are the curly brackets { and } in C++, Java and JavaScript. In Python, we just begin a code block by indenting it, and we end it by no longer indenting.

Python is an interpreted language, which means each line is translated to machine code just before execution. Interpreted languages run slower than compiled languages, but by the late 1990s this didn't matter much, as computers were so powerful. C++'s object code may be small and efficient but coding in Python is quicker. By the turn of the century, the cost of a programmer's time was greater the cost of CPU time. And because Python is interpreted, with a free interpreter available for every platform, it is highly portable. Just like Java, Python is "code once, run anywhere". UK schools using C++, Java, JavaScript or VB gradually moved over to Python, and one exam board, Edexcel, now offers a Python-only programming exam. High-level languages were invented to be more English-like, yet many developed a very non-English syntax full of odd punctuation and structure. Python remains close to English and therefore easy to learn.

Pause here and consider Fertile Question 6: "Why do interpreted languages run slower than compiled languages, and why does this matter less today?"

_____

_____

IDLE hands

IDLE is shipped with Python and is often the first Integrated Development Environment (IDE) a novice programmer encounters. An IDE provides many features to speed up coding, for example IDLE colours keywords orange and literals green to make syntax errors easier to spot. IDEs often provide autocomplete too, which can be annoying, the online IDE "replit.com" is a good example of over-zealous autocomplete! Stepping, breakpoints and variable-tracing all help us debug our programs. Thonny, PyCharm and Mu are popular IDEs for Python; Visual Studio supports C, C++, C#, VB.NET and JavaScript; and Java developers might use Eclipse, NetBeans or IntelliJ IDEA.

TL;DR

Early programming meant manually entering binary codes. Assembly language gave us mnemonics, but we still needed to understand the architecture. The high-level languages Fortran, ALGOL and COBOL abstract away the code from the architecture, letting us use the English keywords IF, WHILE and FOR. A compiler translates this code into machine code, but we need one for every computer system, and because each high-level statement generates multiple machine code instructions, the object code might not be optimal.

Sequence, selection, iteration and subprograms are no accident, but a natural feature of algorithms, and are used in all imperative languages descended from ALGOL, including Pascal, C and Python. Structured code is preferable to "spaghetti code" because it's readable and easy to maintain. C was written by the creator of Unix, and the "hackers' language" evolved into C++ and C#, but its fussy syntax means it's tricky to learn. Universities first taught using Fortran, then Pascal, but in 1981 UK schools went with BASIC as it was already popular on home computers. BASIC inspired Visual Basic, popular in the 1990s and still used today.

Object-oriented programming, beginning with Simula and Smalltalk, gave us classes that are blueprints for objects; each object has attributes and methods and can interact with other objects. This programming style is useful for games programming, but also for modelling, simulation and AI applications. Java was the most popular language around 2000–2015 because it was object-oriented and portable; it could run anywhere thanks to a Java virtual machine created for every popular platform.

Imperative languages like Java, C and Python execute a sequence of instructions. Another paradigm is declarative programming, which comes in two types: functional languages like LISP, Scala and Haskell, and logic languages like Prolog. A functional language describes merely how data is processed by functions. This often results in more elegant code with fewer bugs and is suited to scientific analysis and AI applications.

Code in an interpreted language is translated to machine code line by line, instead of compiled all at once. Perl, JavaScript and Python are all interpreted, allowing rapid coding and testing, which meets the demands of the modern software market. JavaScript is built into browsers to make web pages interactive. Python was launched in 1991 and designed to be fun, simple and flexible. Its clean syntax made it a popular choice for teaching programming.

An understanding of this topic begins with the knowledge that, at its heart, a computer is just a collection of logic circuits that process digital signals of high and low voltages, representing zeros and ones. The circuits are able to decode certain patterns of zeros and ones, and we call these bit patterns "instructions". Each CPU responds to a finite set of these "low-level instructions" – its machine code instruction set.

Coding in binary is difficult and error-prone, so each binary code is given a short, memorable name or mnemonic, such as <Courier New>LDA, SUB <end Courier New>or<Courier New> BRA<end Courier New>. This assembly language is still difficult to code and contains no useful constructs, such as loops or arrays, so high-level languages were invented. High-level languages are more English-like and allow us to write complex programs very quickly. Python, Java, JavaScript, VB.NET, C, C++ and C# are popular high-level languages. Assembly language may still be used where compact code is essential, or for small, mission-critical programs.

High-level code must be translated into machine code before it can be run on the CPU. For this we need a translator. Compilers translate the whole high-level source-code program into machine code, creating an executable file of object code. Interpreters translate the program one line at a time, which allows for rapid coding and debugging but slower execution than compiled code.

An Integrated Development Environment (IDE) is usually used to develop code. An IDE provides many features to speed up coding and debugging, such as syntax-checking, autocomplete, stepping, breakpoints and variable-tracing.

ACT ideas for languages and translators

Now you've read the deep dive, let's do some serious learning activities to consolidate what you have read.

Question It – second attempt!

Answer these now that you have read the content then check against my answers at httcs.online/learn-lang.

1. If we can code in assembly language, with instructions like INP, STA and ADD, why do we need high-level languages?
2. Why are there so many programming languages?
3. Why do video games have a format, such as PC, Xbox, PlayStation?
4. Why did Java become so popular?
5. Can a spreadsheet full of formulas be considered a computer program?
6. Why do interpreted languages run slower than compiled languages, and why does this matter less today?

Stretch It

Choice of language for a purpose

Choose a language with which to code an application for a given purpose. Purposes could include weapons guidance, an online shop, a mobile game, or a new school information system.

✅ Can you compare the relative merits of compiled versus interpreted languages, high-level versus low-level coding, and the development and support models of open-source versus proprietary systems?

Specifying syntax

✅ Describe the syntax of your most familiar programming language. Use English descriptions such as "an assignment statement is written <variable-identifier> = <expression>".

Comparing paradigms

✅ Compare a functional implementation of factorial (see page 89) with a typical imperative one. What are the advantages of each? How might errors creep into the imperative version that could not be coded in the functional one?

Link It

Links to system software, programming, issues

✅ Explore Python's history with the class. Python is an open-source language; its runtime, interpreter and all libraries are freely available online and can be used without charge. Contrast with closed-source compilers such as C#.

Links to architecture, memory, networks, issues

✅ Discuss what makes a programming language successful. Look at trends in programming languages driven by new platforms such as web and mobile. Consider the effect of Moore's law on processor power and cost of memory. How have these trends influenced language popularity over time?

Link to languages

The terms "syntax" and "semantics" were borrowed from the study of natural languages. "Colorless green ideas sleep furiously" is grammatically correct but has no meaning. This sentence was devised by the linguist and cognitive scientist Noam Chomsky in 1955 to illustrate the difference between syntax and semantics.

Here's a Python example of this issue:

```if age > 18: print("come in") else print("no, sorry!")```	```if age >= 18: print("come in") else print("no, sorry")```
This code will output "no, sorry!" if the age entered is exactly 18, because of a semantic or logic error.	This code will behave as expected, with the addition of a single equals sign. Both code samples are syntactically correct.

✅ Write English sentences with syntax errors and with semantic errors.

Correct It

Misconception	Reality
Computers just "understand" code	To run a high-level language, you need a translator program, either an interpreter or compiler, which creates machine code for that computer. The binary machine code is still not "understood" but rather processed by unintelligent logic circuits.
A program is always a set of instructions	This is true of imperative languages, but not true of declarative languages such as LISP, Prolog and Haskell. Unfortunately, we usually teach this misconception as a "necessary evil" from primary school, as the programming paradigms concept is too abstract for that level of learning. In preparation for A-level, we might "unteach" it with brief exposure to functional programming in KS4 (Years 9 and 10).
Python is the only language, or all computers understand Python	Many languages are available. Lack of exposure to different languages causes this. It's a good idea to look briefly at other languages in KS4, e.g. VBA within Excel if your school has Microsoft Office, JavaScript within App Lab at code.org, or the JavaScript W3Schools tutorial.
Java = JavaScript	Explaining the history of both languages should clear up this misconception.
Translators reside in ROM	Translators are system software utilities. Learners often don't realise that compilers and interpreters are system software, and usually not supplied with the operating system but downloaded and installed on secondary storage when needed.

Check It: Language and translators

Concept	Need to learn 😞	Getting there 😐	Mastered 😊
I can describe a CPU instruction set and know that every CPU has a different instruction set.			
I can explain the purpose and properties of low-level languages: • Machine code • Assembly language			
I can explain the need for high-level languages and describe their features.			
I can choose a high- or low-level language for a purpose.			
I can explain translators: their purpose, advantages and disadvantages: • Compiler • Interpreter			
I can describe the purpose and features of an IDE.			

Endnotes

1   Levy, S. (1984) *Hackers: heroes of the computer revolution*, Doubleday

2   Read more about Grace Hopper at Isaac Computer Science: isaaccomputerscience. org/page/grace_hopper

3   Barton, M. and Stedman, C. (2008) "Timeline: the Gates era at Microsoft", *Computerworld*, link.httcs.onlin/gatesletter

4   See Isaac Computer Science for a tutorial on OOP: isaaccomputerscience.org/ concepts/prog_oop_fundamentals

CHAPTER 5. ALGORITHMS

This topic explores how algorithms exist as a concepts before they are implemented as programs on a computer. We look at the most useful algorithms and where they came from.

Question It

Now take a moment to contemplate these questions.

1. What does abstraction have to do with satellite navigation?
2. How did Babbage use pattern-matching?
3. Why are there so many ways to express an algorithm?
4. Why are searching and sorting algorithms so important?
5. Why are there so many different algorithms for the same purpose?

Again, you will be prompted to think about these fertile questions at relevant points within the "Explore It" section, and you will get a second attempt at the end of the section.

Explore It

Too clever by half

"… bad fortune dogged them from that day forward, the village was destroyed seven times by fire, and visited seven times by the king's vengeance. So, in time, it came to pass that the people fell into a wretched plight. They concluded that there must be some breeder of misfortune among them, and resolved to divide into two bands. This they did and there were then two bands of five hundred families each. Thence-forward, ruin dogged the band which included the parents of the future Losaka, whilst the other five hundred families [thrived] apace. So, the former resolved to go on halving their numbers, and did so, until this one family was parted from all the rest. Then they knew that the breeder of misfortune was in that family, and with blows drove them away."

An extract from the Jataka, an ancient Buddhist text.

Abstractions all the way down

In her excellent book *Hello World*, Hannah Fry explains that all algorithms fall into four main categories. Prioritisation algorithms choose the best series of chess moves from the billions of possibilities. Classification algorithms recognise obstacles in front of a self-driving car. Association algorithms match people in dating apps or recommend what to buy next. Filtering algorithms remove noise from sound recordings or stop spam from filling up your inbox.

Finding a route using a mapping service such as Google Maps is an example of prioritisation. Google Maps owes its success to the programming pioneer Edsger Dijkstra. Dijkstra's algorithm first measures all the possible road segments from the start position to the next choice of road. The process is repeated, keeping a running total for each route so far. If any two routes meet, only the shortest route is retained. Once the destination has been reached, only one "winning" route remains.

Of course, Dijkstra's algorithm works on an abstraction of the road network, a simplified diagram that mathematicians call a graph. The graph consists of nodes, edges and edge weights, all stored as numbers in a data structure. Abstracting real world data into a suitable data structure, and then writing a matching algorithm to process it, are the key skills at the heart of programming. You want a program to detect cancer cells in biopsy samples? Get the image data into a suitable abstraction and then write a program to process the data, detecting the patterns of numbers that match indicators for cancer in the image. The first part of the process is data abstraction, which is not just "removing unnecessary detail", it means retaining just the details required to *answer questions* about the data with a suitably matched algorithm.

Algorithmic thinking is required for the second part of the process, which again begins with abstraction. Dijkstra abstracted away any distractions and wrote an algorithm that focuses on checking the distances between nodes and keeping a running total. Abstraction has left us with just the processes required to solve the problem using the abstract data structure.

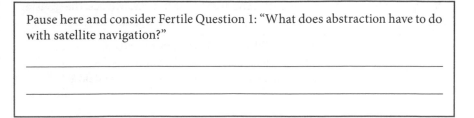

Pause here and consider Fertile Question 1: "What does abstraction have to do with satellite navigation?"

One bite at a time

"There is only one way to eat an elephant: a bite at a time" – proverb

This proverb, popularised by Desmond Tutu, describes another computational thinking skill: decomposition. A routing algorithm finds and joins together multiple short sections to create the complete route. Any sufficiently large problem can be broken down into smaller sub-problems to make it easier to solve.

Nobody taught the German mathematician Carl Friedrich Gauss decomposition, but he was able to use it to great effect from a young age. According to anecdote, Gauss was punished by his primary school teacher with the task of adding the numbers from 1 to 100. The young Gauss was able to compute the sum in a matter of seconds. How?

Gauss had spotted a pattern. Instead of performing $1 + 2 + 3 + \ldots + 98 + 99 + 100$, if he added together the smallest and the largest number, then added together the next numbers inwards, and so on, he would get identical results. For example:

$1 + 100 = 101$

$2 + 99 = 101$

$3 + 98 = 101$

There are 50 such sums, so the answer is just $50 \times 101 = 5050$. Gauss had decomposed a large problem into 50 trivial ones, making the whole problem simple to solve.

Sum of its parts

Charles Babbage's 1820s Difference Engine (see page 21) relied on decomposition to calculate polynomials. To illustrate how this worked, let's take a quick look at the simplest polynomial, $f(x) = x^2$. The results of this function for each value from 1 to 7 are (1,4,9,16,25,36,49).

We now calculate the difference between each pair of consecutive terms, calling this the *first-order difference* (3,5,7,9,11,13). Now calculate the difference *between each difference*, which we call the second-order difference, we see the constant value 2.

x	$f(x) = x^2$	First-order difference (this term minus the previous term) d(x)	Second-order difference (this difference minus the previous difference) constant 2
0	0		
1	1	1	
2	4	3	2
3	9	5	2
4	16	7	2
5	25	9	2
6	36	11	2
7	49	13	2

So, to calculate any term f(x), we can just take the previous term, f(x–1), add the first difference for that term, d(x–1), and then the constant difference of 2:

$$f(x) = f(x–1) + d(x–1) + 2$$

Now calculating 5^2 is a simple matter of addition. The previous term is $4^2=16$. Then we add the previous first difference of 7, making 23, and then the constant difference of 2, making 25.

$$f(5) = f(4) + d(4) + 2$$
$$= 16 + 7 + 2 = 25$$

Babbage had used pattern-matching to see that the difference of squares followed a regular sequence. In fact, a polynomial of any degree will eventually show a constant difference. For example, a function containing x^3 will have a constant third-order difference.

Babbage designed his engine to calculate these differences using a physical column of gears for each column. Each cog held a decimal digit and one whole column stored a 20-digit decimal number. Unfortunately, the precision metalwork needed for the gears to perform reliably was beyond the late Georgian engineers. This scuppered Babbage's attempts to scale the machine to work with powers of seven, so only a version capable of calculating second-order differences was ever built.

Pause here and consider Fertile Question 2: "How did Babbage use pattern-matching?"

_____

_____

The House of Wisdom

The Islamic Golden Age, from around the 8th century to the 14th century, was a period of cultural, economic and scientific flourishing. The caliph Hārūn al-Rashīd (circa 786-809) founded the House of Wisdom in Baghdad, which was the largest city in the world at that time. Islamic scholars from all over the globe gathered there to translate the world's classical knowledge into Arabic and Persian. Among them was Muḥammad ibn Mūsā al-Khwārizmī (circa 780-850), a Persian scholar of mathematics, astronomy and geography. In around 820, al-Khwārizmī was appointed astronomer and head of the library and produced maps of the world, determined the circumference of the Earth and compiled astronomical tables for navigation.

Figure 5.1: Muḥammad ibn Mūsā al-Khwārizmī gave the world algorithms and algebra.

Al-Khwārizmī's work on elementary algebra, _Al-Kitāb al-mukhtaṣar fī ḥisāb al-jabr wa'l-muqābala (The Compendious Book on Calculation by Completion and_

Balancing), was translated into Latin in the 12th century, whereupon the Arabic word "al-jabr" gave the world the term "algebra". Another work, *Al-Khwārizmī Concerning the Hindu Art of Reckoning*, is preserved only in a Latin translation, with the title *Algoritmi de numero Indorum*. From al-Khwārizmī's name came the word "algorithm".

The first programmer

Even before Babbage had finished the Difference Engine he had begun a more ambitious project. The Analytical Engine was to be a general-purpose calculating machine, and with components we would recognise today: the "Mill" as the arithmetic logic unit (ALU) and the "Store" as storage. Although it was never built, Ada Lovelace (see chapter 1) was fascinated by the Analytical Engine's possibilities and wrote her own notes on the machine.

The most famous became known as "Note G", explaining how to "program" the engine to calculate "Bernoulli numbers": highly-prized mathematical constants. Lovelace's program for the machine contains 25 steps and a loop, and she helpfully included a trace table for the eighth Bernoulli number, showing the contents of "variables" at each stage of execution. These notes cement her position in history as the first computer programmer.

> "My Dear Babbage. I am in much dismay at having got into so amazing a quagmire & botheration with these Numbers, that I cannot possibly get the thing done today. ... I am now going out on horseback. Tant mieux" – Ada Lovelace to Charles Babbage, 1843[1]

Drawing an algorithm

Babbage had expressed machine functions in written notes, which he called "mechanical notation". Meanwhile, Lovelace's program used the language of mathematical expressions. Early digital computers in the 1940s would be programmed in binary or "mnemonics" in assembly language. But a husband-and-wife team in New Jersey, US, changed all that.

Lillian Gilbreth, one of the first female engineers to earn a PhD, and her husband, Frank, were efficiency experts. In 1921, they wrote a paper called *Process charts: first steps in finding the one best way to do work*. An early flowchart using the Gilbreths' notation is seen in figure 5.2. Their tools quickly became popular in industrial engineering and later in computer programming.

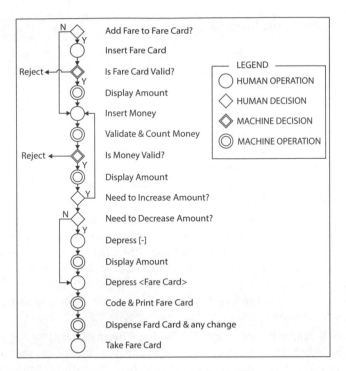

Figure 5.2: An early flowchart created by Lillian and Frank Gilbreth.

The American National Standards Institute set standards for flowcharts and their symbols in the 1960s. The rise of high-level languages and interactive computer terminals later caused flowcharts to fall out of favour. Pseudocode replaced the flowchart when it was still necessary to write an algorithm precisely, in a standard syntax.

Pause here and consider Fertile Question 3: "Why are there so many ways to express an algorithm?"

The last place you look

Some algorithms are so useful that they crop up everywhere. To find a book on an unsorted shelf, we might look at each book in turn, compare with the book we need, until we find it. This is a linear or serial search. "Linear" because the time taken grows in a straight line as the number of items grows. In other words, if a linear search takes one second to search 50 items, then it will take 10 seconds to search 500 items, and 100 seconds to search 5000. We say that it has "linear time complexity"; time is proportional to the number of items n, which we describe in "Big O notation" as O(n). Programs with two nested loops, such as bubble sort, have "polynomial time complexity" of $O(n^2)$, meaning they quickly become slow as the number of items to process increases.

Real-world applications, like web search, need to return results in a fraction of a second from billions of items, and linear search is too slow for this purpose. If we can sort the data first, we can use another algorithm. In binary search we check the midpoint of the array. If this matches our target, stop. If the target is lower than the midpoint, discard the top half of the array; if higher, discard the bottom half. Repeat this process until the target is found. This is called a binary search because we split the list into two parts each time; we bisect it.

Binary search can be demonstrated by playing "Twenty Questions" or the board game Guess Who? Because it's a "divide and conquer" algorithm that halves the search space with each comparison, binary search has logarithmic time complexity. This means it scales well to a large dataset, as long as it's sorted first.

Order, order

Finding, adding or deleting data is much more efficient if the array or database table is in sorted order. Sorting is so important in computer science that there are at least a dozen basic algorithms in common use. Sorting is necessary to keep data organised, and the world creates 2.5 exabytes (2.5 x 10^{18} bytes) of data every day. As we saw earlier, finding useful information requires us to search the data, and sorted data is easier to search. Typical UK GCSE courses look at three sort algorithms: bubble, insertion and merge.

Pause here and consider Fertile Question 4: "Why are searching and sorting algorithms so important?"

_____

_____

Bubble sort is simple to implement but very inefficient. It is so called because each pass over the data, swapping adjacent items, causes the largest item to "bubble" to the top. The two nested loops cause a time complexity of n^2, meaning this algorithm does not scale well to large datasets. Where bubble sort wins, however, is in the small amount of memory needed to run it, we say bubble sort has a low space complexity.

Rather than simply swapping adjacent items, insertion looks at each item in turn, moving it leftwards and inserting it into the correct place. Insertion sort seems like it should be more efficient, but with a worst case of n^2 it is little better than bubble sort. Both bubble and insertion sort are intuitive sorting methods that cannot be attributed to an inventor.

Merge sort, however, was an invention of one of the most brilliant minds in computing history, John von Neumann. After splitting the dataset repeatedly until we get single elements, we combine them into ordered pairs, then fours, and so on until we have a single sorted list. This "divide and conquer" algorithm, like binary search, is highly efficient. Because a list of n items can only be halved $\log_2(n)$ times, there are $\log_2(n)$ stages to a merge sort. Each stage consists of n/2 comparisons, so a merge sort consists of $n/2 * \log_2(n)$ operations. We simplify this expression to $O(n.\log(n))$. This time complexity makes merge sort one of the most efficient sorting algorithms. But it's fiendishly difficult to code compared to bubble sort, and the latter performs better on very short lists or where the data is almost sorted anyway.

Pause here and consider Fertile Question 5: "Why are there so many different algorithms for the same purpose?"

_____

_____

Lost without a trace

Ada Lovelace demonstrated a technique we use to prove the correctness of an algorithm, called a trace table. Some logic errors in our algorithm are not obvious either to the programmer's eye or even after execution. This is where tracing can help. A trace table would drive out logic errors and is often used as part of a "dry run" or walkthrough of the code before execution or during verification. This can be done as part of a code review to drive out security flaws in a program (see chapter 10).

TL;DR

In chapter 2 we saw that programming is not about using the correct keywords "if", "while" and so on. Rather it's the process of solving a problem with the building blocks of code: sequence, selection and iteration. In this chapter, we've seen how algorithms pre-date computer science by thousands of years, and derive largely from mathematics and the natural sciences. Indeed, the word "algorithm" comes from the name of a Persian scholar, Muhammad ibn Mūsā al-Khwārizmī (circa 780-850). It's important to understand that an algorithm exists as a concept in its own right, and that a program is merely the implementation of an algorithm on a computer. The key processes involved in creating an algorithm are abstraction, decomposition and logical thinking.

Some algorithms are so useful they crop up again and again, so an understanding of searching and sorting algorithms is necessary in computer science. Two or more algorithms can be created to solve the same problem, and they will perform differently given the same inputs, so it's important to choose the right algorithm for a task. Learners should be able to identify algorithms, interpret their purpose from flowcharts and pseudocode, correct errors and complete unfinished algorithms. To help with all this, they should be able to trace an algorithm that also drives out logic errors.

Question It – second attempt!

Answer these now that you have read the content, then check against my answers at httcs.online/learn-algo.

1. What does abstraction have to do with satellite navigation?
2. How did Babbage use pattern-matching?
3. Why are there so many ways to express an algorithm?

4.   Why are searching and sorting algorithms so important?

5.   Why are there so many different algorithms for the same purpose?

ACT ideas for algorithms

In this section we explore some valuable learning activities you can carry out related to algorithms.

ACT key skill: mind mapping

When I was looking for a way of organising my work life in the 1990s, I came across a book by British psychology author and TV presenter Tony Buzan called *Use Your Head*. It was my first introduction to mind maps and I have never looked back!

A mind map is a diagram that displays a collection of knowledge around a central idea. You can learn more here: link.httcs.online/mindmaps.

☑   Make a mind map of the key topics in the algorithms topic now. Use the PLC at the end of this chapter to prompt you if stuck. Compare your mind map to mine at httcs.online/algo.

Stretch It

Making computational thinking explicit

☑   Try to "label" your work with the computational thinking (CT) skills used, as they use them. For example, if you are writing an algorithm to calculate train fares, based on number of stations travelled, you will use abstraction, decomposition and algorithmic thinking. Name these processes as you use them. Get your teacher to help with this if you feel stuck.

Matching the algorithm to the data structure

Information in the real world can be abstracted into a data structure in many ways.

☑   Consider the ways in which routing data for a satnav or train station data can be abstracted for use by an algorithm. How many ways could we store this data? For example, an array, a list, records in a table, a linked list. Explore the algorithms needed to process the different data structures and see how a different algorithm has to be devised for each data structure.

Seeing the complexity in the code

Bubble sort has "polynomial" time complexity, $O(n^2)$. Look at the pseudocode for the algorithm and determine why this is. Explore the relationship between the code and the time complexity and suggest tweaks that can be made to bring down the average execution time. A discussion of sorting algorithms, including use of a Boolean flag to control the outer loop to achieve this, is available at geeksforgeeks.org.

Complexity, exponents and logarithms

Binary search and merge sort are "divide and conquer" algorithms.

☑ Find out what this means and why it causes the algorithms to have logarithmic complexity. Discuss logarithms and their relationship to number bases. Binary search is $O(\log_2(n))$ because $\log_2(n)$ answers the question "How many times can the number n be halved until we reach 1?" Realise that this happens exactly because $2^a = n$ implies $a = \log_2(n)$. Explore the relationship between exponent, logarithm and number base with your maths teacher or online at link.httcs. online/logarithms.

Relate It

Visualisation websites

The excellent visualgo.net was created by a professor at the National University of Singapore. It demonstrates the major sorting algorithms in a visual way.

YouTube resources

You may already be familiar with the "Hungarian folk dancers" sorting videos at link.httcs.online/bubbledance, while Tom Scott from the Computerphile YouTube channel explains Big O notation on his own channel at link.httcs.online/bigo.

Link It

Link to architecture

☑ Explore computer benchmarking, the process of determining how well a computer performs when given different algorithms to run. If you can, run the same program on different computers and compare the results. Consider what this means, with respect to the CPU cores, clock and cache size, and the memory available to the different machines. Pseudocode samples for various algorithms are available at isaaccomputerscience.org.

Link to data and networks

☑ Explore compression algorithms and why they are important in streaming services. Find out about run-length encoding and discuss with your teacher or a study partner why it's not suitable for video-streaming. Explore JPEG compression and dictionary techniques, and compare their effectiveness on different data.

☑ Once you understand where the Big O formula comes from, can you determine the time complexities of different solutions from the code? If you are a strong programmer, you could challenge yourself to improve an algorithm or even devise your own compression algorithm for images or text.

Link to issues and impacts

Algorithms such as cryptocurrency miners are in the news because they use huge amounts of energy to carry out their complex calculations. It's said that bitcoin alone now has the energy consumption of Argentina.

☑ Discuss the ethical implications of computationally expensive algorithms with your classmates.

Link to science

Once familiar with the skills, look out for where you might use CT in problem-solving outside computer science, perhaps in other school subjects or daily life. For example, in biology you might be asked to devise an experiment to test for starch. You would abstract from all the properties of starch just the important property: iodine attaches to starch and dyes it blue. You must then decompose the problem into steps: set up apparatus, run experiment, gather data, analyse, write conclusion. Then you might write an algorithm for the step-by-step process.

☑ Noticing where CT is being used in other subjects like this helps make it familiar to you. Maybe you can even explain it to your science teacher!

Unplug It

Linear search is very common, so it would be easy to act this out in the classroom or anywhere with playing cards, books or people. Binary search can be demonstrated with a simple "high-low" guessing game: one player chooses a number from 1 to 63, and another tries to identify it in the lowest number of guesses, guided only by "higher" or "lower". The guesser should be able to get it right in six attempts every time if they operate the binary search algorithm correctly. There are lots more binary search activities at csunplugged.org.

Build It

Writing algorithms for maze-solving robots is an excellent physical computing activity to practise CT and explore optimisation algorithms. These activities are perfect for cross-curricular learning with science and design and technology, and for project work. Many tutorials are available online.

☑ Even if you can't get physical, you can write maze-solving programs in Scratch. A project you can remix to get started is described at "Pops' Scratch blog" at link.httcs.online/scratchmaze.

Correct It

Misconception	Reality
Pseudocode has a specific syntax	Pseudocode follows the basic structure of a programming language but has no specific syntax. UK assessment authorities have clouded the issue by publishing "pseudocode syntax" guides and requiring exam answers in specific formats. Always use terms like "exam reference language" to distinguish these from pseudocode.
An algorithm is a flowchart, piece of pseudocode or program	Flowcharts, pseudocode and programs are all different representations of an algorithm that exists as a concept in its own right. A program is the implementation of an algorithm on a computer as an automatic process.

Two items in an array can be swapped with two assignment statements, one to copy left, and one to copy right, such as:
 `a[i] = a[i+1]`
 `a[i+1] = a[i]`
	A temporary variable is needed to store one of the values, otherwise it will be lost when overwritten by the first assignment statement.
	
	 ``` temp = a[i] a[i] = a[i+1] a[i+1] = temp ```
	 Misconceptions like this arise because of the weakness of the learner's understanding of program execution. It is helpful to develop their understanding of a "notional machine" (see chapter 2).
	
	 NB: Python (like some other languages) does allow assignment of values to multiple variables in one line, so you can write this code, but this is not the same as the misconception noted.
	
	 `a[i], a[i+1] = a[i+1], a[i]`
	 In this statement, each of the two expressions on the right of the equals sign are evaluated and then assigned to the elements on the left. Therefore, this code will successfully swap two array elements in one line.

When running a sort algorithm, the computer can "see" all the elements at once and therefore place an element in the correct place in a single operation	A program can only compare two values, so, for example, in insertion sort, the current item must be compared with each item on its left until correctly placed. This can mean many comparisons. This misconception arises during teaching of sort algorithms, when the whole array is visible to the learners at one time. We can head this off by using animation that hides all the elements, only revealing an element when the algorithm "looks" at it. The NCCE curriculum resources include just such an animation.[2]

Misconception	Reality
Standard algorithms have a single, correct programmatic implementation	Standard algorithms are concepts. They describe the basic operation of a process, but the detailed implementation of an algorithm can vary. For example, when implementing binary search, it does not matter whether, on finding the mid-point in a sublist with an even number of elements, we go left or right. Neither choice is the correct one, and the implementation is usually arbitrary. Quick sort (which we meet at A-level) repeatedly sorts the data into two sublists either side of a "pivot". The choice of pivot is again arbitrary, although some books suggest the first element, while some suggest the middle element of the array. Neither choice is more correct than the other.

Check It: Algorithms

Concept	Need to learn 😞	Getting there 😐	Mastered 😊
I know that an algorithm is a precise, ordered series of steps to solve a problem constructed of sequence, selection and iterations.			
I know how to choose an algorithm for a task.			
I can explain why algorithm performance can vary depending on the input data.			
I know that multiple algorithms exist to solve the same problem, and can explain why they will perform differently given the same input data.			
I know that algorithms can be represented in many ways, including flowcharts, pseudocode and program code.			
I can create representations of algorithms in flowcharts, pseudocode and program code.			
I know the characteristics of, and can recognise the representations of these common algorithms: bubble sort, insertion sort, merge sort, linear search and binary search.			
I can interpret, complete, correct and trace algorithms using a trace table.			

Endnotes

1   King, G. (2015) "How Ada Lovelace solved problems", *Solvitas Perambulum* (blog), link.httcs.online/tantmieux

2   link.httcs.online/nccebubble

CHAPTER 6. ARCHITECTURE

This topic covers the history of computer hardware and how it hangs together, and why all computers perform a fetch-decode-execute cycle first described by John von Neumann in 1945.

Question It

First take a moment to contemplate these questions.

1. Where did the idea of an instruction cycle of Fetch-Decode and Execute come from?

2. Do modern computers have a Von Neumann or a Harvard architecture?

3. Why don't we make the cache huge and get rid of RAM and secondary storage?

4. Why is Moore's law slowing down and what can we do about it?

5. What innovation helped ARM chips take over the world?

6. What do the Manchester Baby and the iPhone still have in common?

Again, you will be prompted to think about these fertile questions at relevant points within the deep dive, and you will get a second attempt at the end of the section.

Explore It

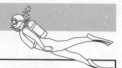

Friends, series 2, episode 8, "The One With the List" (1995)

Chandler: All right, check out this bad boy. Twelve megabytes of RAM, 500-megabyte hard drive. Built-in spreadsheet capabilities and a modem that transmits at over 28,000 bps.

Phoebe: Wow. What are you gonna use it for?

Chandler: Games and stuff.

We may laugh, looking back now at Chandler's "cutting-edge laptop", but that quote illustrates "Moore's law". The laptop I'm writing this book on has 8GB RAM, a 500GB hard drive and 300 Mbps wireless networking, making it roughly a thousand times more powerful while costing less than a tenth of the price of Chandler's. In 1965, electronics pioneer Gordon Moore noted in an article in the 35th anniversary edition of *Electronics* magazine that computing power was doubling every two years.[1] Moore's law remained largely reliable until recent years, when chip manufacturers began to hit limits imposed by physics, like the wavelength of the UV lasers used to etch the silicon. Manufacturers are even grappling with "quantum tunnelling" – electrons simply "jumping the gate" when transistors become too small.

But we're getting ahead of ourselves. Long before Chandler's laptop, and two decades before Gordon Moore made his famous prediction, a Hungarian-American scientist was grappling with the complex mathematics of nuclear explosions.

The "think animal"

John von Neumann is known for the arrangement of CPU, register, buses and memory that bears his name – the von Neumann architecture – but he also made great leaps in mathematics, physics and economics, giving the world the phrase "zero-sum game". A child prodigy, von Neumann could divide eight-digit numbers in his head at the age of six, and was described by Albert Einstein as a *Denktier*, meaning "think animal".

Von Neumann worked at the US Army nuclear weapons research base in Los Alamos, New Mexico, on mathematics for the "Fat Man" bomb, the type dropped on the Japanese city of Nagasaki on 9 August 1945. Frustrated with slow IBM mechanical tabulating machines (see chapter 3), he designed a new general purpose machine called the EDVAC.

EDVAC would contain the internal components we would recognise today: arithmetic unit, control unit, clock, main memory, input/output manager and secondary storage. Using a cycle of "fetch, decode and execute", the same memory store could be used for both instructions and data. EDVAC was built in 1949 to replace a simpler machine called ENIAC. It was a digital, stored-program computer, but it wasn't the first.

Pause here and consider Fertile Question 1: "Where did the idea of an instruction cycle of Fetch-Decode and Execute come from?"

_____

_____

Baby steps

Freddie Williams had already successfully built a prototype CRT memory (see chapter 1) in 1946, when he took up the chair of electrical engineering at Manchester University, UK. Familiar with von Neumann's work, Williams thought his own tube memory would make an ideal random-access store for a von Neumann computer and built one with Tom Kilburn and Geoff Tootill. In June 1948, the Small-Scale Experimental Machine, also known as the Manchester Baby, successfully calculated the highest proper factor of the number 2^{18} (answer 262,144) in just 52 minutes.

The Baby used more than 500 valves, was five metres long and weighed around a tonne, but had a von Neumann architecture that we would recognise today. Other early computers were ground-breaking in their own ways but limited in others. Bletchley Park's Colossus (see chapter 10) was electronic, but ran only a few specialised programs set up by a plugboard. ENIAC was "programmed" via switches and cables because it had no program memory. So the Manchester Baby has the honour of being the first fully electronic, stored-program, general purpose computer.

The Baby could fetch, decode and execute around 700 instructions per second. Through a 3-bit binary code, just seven instructions were available, including subtraction.

To save on logic circuitry, addition was performed using negating and subtraction, which works because a + b is the same as – (– a – b). A replica Baby was constructed in 1998 and is on display in the Science and Industry Museum in Manchester.

Figure 6.1: The Manchester Baby was the first fully electronic, stored-program, general purpose computer.

Mark 1

In 1948, Turing joined the team at Manchester and helped design the more ambitious Mark 1 computer. This machine still used CRT memory, but now performed addition and logical comparisons in an expanded set of 30 instructions. Crucially, a newly developed magnetic drum added secondary storage for the first time. The Manchester Mark 1 became the world's first commercial computer, the Ferranti Mark 1, in February 1951.

Like the ENIAC and the EDVAC, the Mark 1 was programmed by a team of women – among them Mary Lee Berners-Lee, whose son Tim would go on to invent the World Wide Web (see chapter 9). Ferranti sold nine Mark 1s publicly and an unknown number to government agencies, before switching to newly invented transistors to make the Atlas supercomputer in 1962.

Evergreen design

From the Manchester Baby to the modern day, the design of a general-purpose computer has changed little.

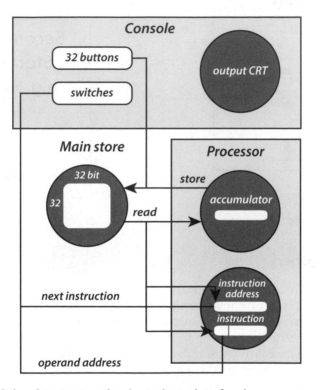

Figure 6.2: Baby's architecture is strikingly similar to that of modern computers.

Figure 6.2 shows a schematic of the Baby. We can see the processor (ALU) and three registers that are familiar to us: accumulator, instruction address (which we know as the program counter) and instruction register (or current instruction register). We see a main store (RAM) and the lines connecting the processor to the main store (buses). And at the top, we see the input devices (buttons and switches) and output device (output CRT). Figure 6.3, created by William Lau, is the schematic of a modern computer, showing the same registers and buses. With the addition of a few more registers, this is clearly the same design.

Computer Systems - Von Neumann Architecture

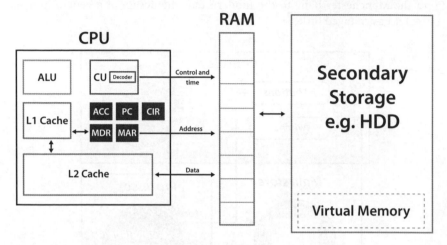

Figure 6.3: The architecture of a modern computer.

Bottle openers

Early computers were largely limited by the processing speed of the CPU. In the 1960s, however, fast-switching transistors changed all this: suddenly CPUs were sitting idle, waiting for instructions or data. Splitting main storage into data memory and instruction memory allowed the CPU to fetch an instruction on one bus, while simultaneously fetching data on another. This twin-memory solution to the "Von Neumann bottleneck" is sometimes known as the Harvard architecture. Modern computers combine von Neumann and Harvard ideas in a "hybrid architecture" to maximise performance.

> Pause here and consider Fertile Question 2: "Do modern computers have a Von Neumann or a Harvard architecture?"
>
> _____
>
> _____

The three Cs

The Manchester Baby worked at around 700 instructions per second. By the time *Friends'* Chandler bought his laptop in 1995, affordable CPUs ran at 25 MHz or 25 million instructions per second – up by a factor of 40,000 in 48 years. The CPU in your laptop probably runs at over 2 GHz, which is three million times the speed of the Baby. As valves gave way to transistors, which were then miniaturised into integrated circuits, the shrinking size and power consumption of the silicon allowed clock speeds to increase. As the electrons have shorter distances to travel, the logic gates can all do their stuff in a shorter time period, and the clock can tick over faster. The first C of performance is, therefore, clock speed.

Remember that the CPU waits idly for instructions or data a lot of the time. Pulling bits across the system bus from RAM is relatively slow. Even at the speed of electricity (which is close to the speed of light), a fetch from RAM can take 100 nanoseconds – a whopping 200 clock ticks of wasted processing time.

In order to speed up execution of programs, instructions can be cached. Cache memory responds in as little as one nanosecond or just two CPU cycles. When cache holds both instructions and data, that code completes far quicker than if it were all in RAM. Cache is the second of the three Cs, which improves a computer's performance.

Why don't we make all main memory into cache? The answer is that cache is expensive and, ironically, the bigger it gets, the slower it performs. All CPUs since Intel's 8086 (released in 1978) therefore contain technology that prefetches contents from RAM into cache to prevent CPU idleness. Processors now have many levels of cache: a tiny level 1 cache tightly integrated with the CPU has lightning performance, while level 2 and sometimes level 3 are further away, relatively slower and cheaper.

> Pause here and consider Fertile Question 3: "Why don't we make the cache huge and get rid of RAM and secondary storage?"
>
> _____
>
> _____

We can further increase performance by making CPUs with two or more processing cores on one silicon wafer. In May 2005, AMD's Athlon 64 X2 was launched as the first commercial dual-core CPU. Multitasking operating systems like Windows can give CPU time to two programs at once, with each core running its own fetch-decode-execute cycle. Some programs, such as games and video-rendering software, can even run two parts of the same program simultaneously – a trick called multithreading. Today's home computers usually have two or four cores, and Apple's iPhone 8 and X models have six. Number of cores is the third C in our discussion of computer performance characteristics.

> Pause here and consider Fertile Question 4: "Why is Moore's law slowing down and what can we do about it?"
>
> _____
>
> _____

Remembering stuff

Before Williams tubes, computer memory usually consisted of slow magnetic drums, slower tapes or cumbersome "acoustic delay lines". Developed from radar technology, a delay line carried pulses of sound representing binary data through a tube of fluid, usually mercury. A pulse reaching the end is detected, carried electrically back to the beginning and retransmitted. This constant loop of pulses allowed the Cambridge EDSAC delay lines to each "hold" a pattern of 560 bits. Of course, mercury is heavy. Figure 6.3 shows a device providing just 1.5 KB of memory, needing 18 mercury tubes which weighed in at nearly 800lbs, or a third of a tonne.[2] The sound waves bouncing around the device sounded like human voices, earning it the nickname "mumble-tub".[3]

Figure 6.4: Pulses of sound bounced back and forth in the UNIVAC's "mumble-tub" mercury delay line memory.

Tape and delay-line memory were both serial access devices, meaning the bits you wanted had to come back around before you could read them. Williams' fully electronic CRT memory allowed for random access, making Turing's stored-program computer a possibility. No longer tied to paper tapes, plugboards and cumbersome delay-line memory, electronic computers took off.

Random thoughts

RAM allowed programs to include loops and branching at no extra performance cost. Therefore, along with the three Cs, RAM capacity is the fourth major characteristic affecting computer performance. We heard earlier that the Manchester Baby 128 bytes of memory. But Williams tubes were highly sensitive to environmental disturbances, so more robust solutions were sought.

The mid-1950s saw the arrival of ferrite core memory. The DEC PDP-1 – on which the first computer game, Spacewar!, was written in 1959 by the MIT hackers – had around 9KB of core memory and IBM's flagship 360 mainframes shipped with up to 6MB of core memory in the late 1960s. The Apollo spacecraft carried around 32KB of core memory (see figure 6.5). Core memory dominated for two decades from the mid-1950s, until semiconductor "dynamic random-access memory" (DRAM) chips became affordable.

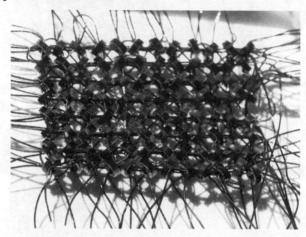

Figure 6.5: Core rope memory was used in NASA's Mariner and Apollo programmes.

Never let me go

DRAM, like the Williams tube, is volatile: it loses its contents when powered off. Core memory was non-volatile, but, of course, it could be altered at any time, so important programs might be overwritten. If the start-up instructions are overwritten it's *game over* for that computer, so we need memory that cannot be altered, known as read-only memory (ROM).

The 1970s semiconductor industry made a series of breakthroughs in ROM design, culminating in "EEPROM" chips that could be cheaply programmed and reprogrammed in the computer factory. By the mid-1970s, all electronic computers shipped with semiconductor RAM and ROM.

Because RAM and ROM are accessible directly by the CPU, they are known collectively as main memory or primary storage. ROM is non-volatile, but we can't write to it. RAM is volatile, so contents are lost on power off. Another type of storage is necessary to keep the data we create, and to store programs permanently.

Forget me not

Secondary storage is non-volatile, writeable storage. Early secondary stores were often magnetic. The IBM 305 RAMAC computer shipped in 1956 with just a 4MB magnetic hard drive for secondary storage. Modern desktop PC magnetic hard drives now exceed one terabyte (TB) – that's one million, million bytes. Magnetic tape drives were also used commercially up to the turn of the century, when cloud storage and flash memory made them largely obsolete.

Early home computers shipped with their operating systems in ROM and just a floppy drive for storage, until small hard drives became affordable in the 1990s. A floppy was a thin flexible disk coated in magnetic material, encased in hard plastic that stored just 1.4 megabytes. Although they are now obsolete, the "save" icon in many current software programs still resembles a floppy disk.

Solid state storage has started replacing magnetic media. The main drawback to all the above examples of magnetic storage is their reliance on moving parts. This movement causes wear and tear, and all magnetic media fails eventually. Solid state drives and USB memory sticks are more resilient to drops and knocks as both contain just silicon chips called flash memory. But beware: although flash memory is physically robust, this "program/erase" cycle degrades the silicon, causing SSDs to fail eventually.

Optical disks complete the set of three main types of secondary storage in common usage. CDs, DVDs and Blu-ray disks consist of a plastic disk pressed with indentations called "pits" – or, in the case of recordable disks, a dye coating that is made reflective in places. These pits (or changes of reflectiveness) are read as binary data by a laser. Optical disks were hugely popular for the distribution of music, video and software throughout the 1990s and 2000s, until downloads and streaming services became available.

The right to bear ARMs

In 1983, Steve Furber and Sophie Wilson at Acorn had just built the BBC Micro (see previous chapters) and were working on a more powerful business machine. They wanted to compete with the Apple Lisa but were unimpressed with the CPUs available, so designed their own chip based on cutting-edge ideas coming out of the University of California, Berkeley.

The falling cost of RAM meant programs didn't have to be tiny anymore. Instruction sets could shrink in size while programs grew. The resulting RISC (reduced instruction set computer) chips carried far fewer logic gates, making them faster and less power-hungry. Wilson was able to imagine the whole circuit for Acorn's new chip all at once, then write a simulation of it in 800 lines of BBC Basic. The Acorn co-founder Hermann Hauser recalled: "While IBM spent months simulating their instruction sets on large mainframes, Sophie did it all in her brain."

Figure 6.6: The ARM processor, seen here in an early test rig, was designed by Sophie Wilson and Steve Furber in Cambridge, UK.

The Acorn RISC Machine (ARM) chip was designed to improve the performance of desktop microcomputers, not to save power and space. But when Apple needed a low-power, cool-running chip for its ill-fated Newton handheld computer in 1987, they chose the ARM. Apple got behind Acorn and in 1990 they spun off the ARM company. After the ARM-powered iPod was launched in 2001, the world went ARM-crazy. By 2010, more than 95% of smartphones contained an ARM processor and the company shipped more than 20 billion chips in 2017.

Pause here and consider Fertile Question 5: "What innovation helped ARM chips take over the world?"

_____

_____

Plus ça change

When we look back at the history of computer architecture, the rapid pace of change is startling. But possibly more fascinating is that the underlying architecture has changed little, despite huge advances in technology. Alan Turing and John von Neumann would recognise the design of today's computers, read the instruction set of the x86 family of processors or the ARM RISC chip and be able to code for it. The genius of the codebreaker and the vision of the *Denktier* live on.

> Pause here and consider Fertile Question 6: "What do the Manchester Baby and the iPhone still have in common?"
>
> _____
>
> _____

TL;DR

Alan Turing described the concept of a stored-program computer in 1936. John von Neumann built on Turing's work, explaining in 1945 how a cycle of fetch-decode-execute could allow the same memory to hold programs and data. Freddie Williams led a team at Manchester University that built the Baby, to prove his CRT memory store. The Baby ran around 700 instructions per second in 1946. Its success led to the 1951 Ferranti Mark 1 – the first commercial computer, for which women wrote most of the programs.

Valves gave way to much faster transistors in the 1960s and this exposed the "von Neumann bottleneck", solved by the Harvard architecture of separate memories for instructions and data. Early memory stores included paper tape, magnetic tape, magnetic drum, acoustic delay lines and core rope memory, until semiconductor RAM arrived in the 1960s.

Magnetic hard disk drives provided secondary storage from the 1950s onwards, with flash memory becoming popular in the 21st century for portable storage devices and solid-state disks (SSDs). Compact discs (CDs), invented in 1979, and DVDs and Blu-ray discs are examples of the third common storage type, the optical disk.

Computer performance is limited by the three Cs: clock speed, number of cores and size of cache. CPUs can be described as CISC (complex instruction set computer) or RISC (reduced instruction set computer). RISC processors have much simpler circuitry, reducing space and power consumption, making them suitable for mobile devices. The ARM chip is a RISC processor used in 95% of all the world's mobile devices.

From the Baby to ARM, all CPUs still contain an ALU, registers and a control unit, and perform a fetch-decode-execute cycle first described by von Neumann in 1945.

ACT ideas for architecture

Question It – second attempt!

Answer these now that you have read the content.

1. Where did the idea of an instruction cycle of Fetch-Decode and Execute come from?
2. Do modern computers have a Von Neumann or a Harvard architecture?
3. Why don't we make the cache huge and get rid of RAM and secondary storage?
4. Why is Moore's law slowing down and what can we do about it?
5. What innovation helped ARM chips take over the world?
6. What do the Manchester Baby and the iPhone still have in common?

ACT key skill: retrieval practice

We discussed retrieval practice in the Introduction and Chapter 1. If you regularly challenge yourself to recall key facts, they will become lodged in long-term memory, and you will remember them when needed.

As well as Quizlet (see chapter 1) there are lots of ways of organising this. Ask your teacher to do lots of "low-stakes quizzing" or subscribe to one of the computer science revision websites. Some of them are: revisecs.computerscienceuk.com, eedi.com and educake.co.uk, but my favourite by far comes from Craig 'n' Dave, the creators of the free video lessons beloved by many CS teachers!

✅ Visit smartrevise.online to sign up for access to thousands of questions or persuade your teacher to get it and you can compete with the class to answer the most questions.

Stretch It

Design a computer
☑ Consider the factors that determine the performance of a computer system, and the characteristics of different types of secondary storage, then design computers for different tasks such as:

- A student taking notes in lectures, studying and writing essays.
- Mining cryptocurrency.
- Navigation by soldiers on the battlefield.

Relate It

Window shopping
☑ Browse computers for sale on shopping websites and discuss the meaning of their characteristics.

Evaporating RAM
☑ Look up the meaning of volatile in the fields of English, chemistry and psychology. How can this help you remember its meaning in computing?

Remember Venn
☑ Categorising the storage types and locations with a Venn diagram can help you grasp the difference between internal/external and primary/secondary.

Link It

Link to languages and programming
Experience of low-level programming, using a simulator such as the Little Man Computer, is an excellent way of learning the architecture of a computer and how it relates to the languages and programming topics.

Link to issues and impacts
Look at the performance of a computer and remember Moore's law. What are the ethical issues with customers perpetually wanting to upgrade their computers and smartphones?

Link to system software
☑ Discuss with your classmates or a study partner how the amount of RAM and CPU determines computer performance. Then link to the process scheduler that gives programs a time slice in rotation in order to share the CPU time fairly.

Also discuss the memory manager that shares out the RAM and swaps programs to virtual memory when necessary.

✅ Consider defragmentation utilities and why they might be needed, particularly with a small hard drive.

Link to data representation
✅ Explore the size of RAM, cache and secondary storage in your computer. What does this means for file sizes that can be held in memory or stored on the hard disk?

Links to history
The architecture of the computer evolved rapidly during the Second World War, out of necessity.

✅ Consider the role of computers in the war: the UK's "Ultra" codebreakers and the US's nuclear Manhattan Project. Speculate about what might have happened without computers – would the war have ended differently?

Links to geography
✅ The ARM chip made mobile computing possible. What impact has this had on global communication?

Unplug It

✅ Role-playing the components of a computer is a great way to help you understand the fetch-decode-execute cycle. You can find an activity called "fetch-decode-execute-plot" at the STEM Learning website,[4] described as "a frantic starter activity aimed at students aged 17-18". Craig 'n' Dave make a similar game available as part of their premium resource pack.[5] Ask your teacher to run this in class!

Build It

✅ The Raspberry Pi is a great way to get hands-on with a small computer. On a Pi or on a Pi image, locate the CPU, RAM and SD-card secondary storage. If possible, open an old desktop computer and compare the two.

Apply It

The ideal project to help you learn computer architecture is to build a desktop computer from components.

✅ If your school runs an after-school club, ask the teacher if you can do this. Your school may well have enough old kit already! There are many tutorials online, including on the Instructables website.[6]

Correct It

Misconception	Reality
Virtual memory is cloud storage	Virtual memory is a space on the hard drive used to extend the available RAM.
Primary = internal Secondary = external	Primary storage is always internal to the computer, but secondary storage can be internal (e.g. main HDD/SSD) or external (portable SSD/HDD or memory stick).
Cache = registers	Cache is general purpose memory. Registers are special purpose stores that hold only a few bytes each and include the PC, MAR, MDR and accumulator. NB: some teaching resources get the registers and cache confused.
Primary = volatile	Primary storage includes RAM, ROM and cache. What makes it primary is that the CPU can read it directly, during the FDE cycle. ROM is, of course, non-volatile.
More secondary storage improves performance	More RAM can sometimes improve performance, but not more secondary storage.
RAM always increases performance	More RAM will not increase performance if there is not a shortage of RAM in the first place. If virtual memory is rarely used, adding RAM won't help.
Secondary storage is used when the RAM is full	Secondary storage is not an extension of RAM – it is long-term non-volatile storage. It holds the operating system and application programs. Virtual memory is a special case, and learners should be clear that this does not mean secondary storage exists for when the RAM is full. Only the start-up instructions reside in ROM in modern computers; the rest of the programs are on secondary storage.
A smartphone is an embedded system	Smartphones are general purpose computers because they run many different applications. Note that a smartwatch is also commonly considered a general-purpose computer, as they usually run apps.
A 3GHz performs better than a 2GHz CPU	There are too many factors at play in the performance of a computer to make this assertion. You need to consider the program(s) it will run and their suitability for multithreading, how much input/output they perform, how much memory they need to run, and whether any processes are suitable for delegating to a co-processor such as a graphics processor unit (GPU). Other factors to consider include the number of cores, size of cache and amount of RAM.
RISC is better than CISC (or vice versa)	RISC processors are generally smaller and consume less power, but require extra RAM and more complex software. The two CPU architectures are suitable for different applications – neither is universally better than the other.

Check It: Architecture

Concept	Need to learn 😞	Getting there 😐	Mastered 😊
I can explain the difference between embedded and general-purpose computers.			
I can describe the architecture of a computer system.			
I can name the parts of a CPU.			
The fetch-decode-execute cycle and the roles of the parts of a CPU during the cycle.			
Primary memory and the characteristics of RAM, ROM and cache.			
The need for secondary storage; types of secondary storage: optical, magnetic, solid state, cloud.			
Volatile versus non-volatile storage.			

Endnotes

1   Moore, G. E. (1965) "Cramming more components onto integrated circuts", *Electronics*, 38(8)

2   link.httcs.online/delayline

3   Fantel, H. H. (1956) "The electronic mind – how it remembers", *Popular Electronics*, link.httcs.online/mumble

4   link.httcs.online/stemfde

5   craigndave.org/a-level-premium-resources

6   link.httcs.online/computerbuild

CHAPTER 7. LOGIC

This topic covers Boolean Logic and how it is used inside a computer to provide arithmetic and logic capabilities.

Question It

Now take a moment to contemplate these questions:

1. Why do computers use binary?
2. What's inside the ALU?
3. How is selection performed inside a computer?
4. Why don't we use analogue computers anymore?
5. How does a computer perform arithmetic?

Again, you will be prompted to think about these fertile questions at relevant points within the deep dive, and you will get a second attempt at the end of the section.

Explore It

An old joke about logic...

A mathematician, a physicist and an astronomer were travelling north by train. They had just crossed the border into Scotland when the astronomer looked out of the window and saw a single black sheep in the middle of a field. "All Scottish sheep are black", he remarked.

"No, my friend," replied the physicist. "Some Scottish sheep are black."

The mathematician looked up from his paper and glanced out of the window. After a few seconds' thought, he said blandly, "In Scotland, there exists at least one field, in which there exists at least one sheep, at least one side of which is black."

Little lightbulbs

When the Bletchley Park team needed to crack the German Lorenz cipher, Tommy Flowers built a computer using 1600 valves. But valves were notoriously unreliable. As in tungsten lightbulbs, the filament inside would fail owing to the stress of repeated expansion and contraction. Fortunately, researchers in New Jersey, US, provided a solution, although they were not working on computers at the time.

Crystal tips

A team at Bell Labs were trying to build an improved amplifier: a fundamental electronic circuit used in radio and telephone equipment. William Shockley believed he could build a "solid state" amplifier without any temperamental valves. Shockley's team glued contacts of gold leaf to a wedge of germanium crystal. Adding a small voltage at the base caused electrons to fill up the gaps in the crystal, allowing a much larger voltage to flow between the gold contacts. Shockley demonstrated the device by using it to amplify speech on 23 December 1947. Combining the words "transfer" and "resistor", Shockley and his team would receive the Nobel Prize for the invention of the "transistor".

Tom Kilburn at Manchester University again led the way with the "Transistor Computer" in 1953. But it still used a number of valves, meaning Bell Labs' 1954 TRADIC was the first fully transistorised computer. In 1959, DEC made the PDP-1 entirely with transistors, and by the late 1960s nobody was using valves.

On and off

Computer scientists quickly realised the transistor's importance as a fast switch. As we saw in chapter 1, computers store and process binary numbers as electrical signals. The transistor allows a 5V signal to be turned on and off electronically at lightning speed, without relays or valves. Representing "True" or "1" as a high voltage, and "False" or "0" as a low voltage, humble transistors can be combined to make logic gates, and those logic gates can be arranged to perform arithmetic.

Pause here and consider Fertile Question 1: "Why do computers use binary?"

Making choices

Imagine you are a parent and your daughter, Ada, asks for a birthday party. You decide to reward good choices and reply, "You can have a party if you tidy your room and do all your homework." You are operating a logic gate with two inputs, which we can call "tidy_room" and "homework". If we call the output "party", we can write the decision like this:

party = tidy_room AND homework

Two transistors connected in series (see figure 7.1) could make the decision for us. Applying a voltage to the base of one transistor if Ada tidies her room, and to the other if she does her homework, we will get a 5V output from the circuit only if Ada does both tasks. We've built the AND logic gate from two transistors. We can combine transistors in other ways to create different logic gates, which are the building blocks of computer circuits.

Pause here and consider Fertile Question 2: "What's inside the ALU?"

The theory behind logic circuits goes back thousands of years, but we can thank a schoolmaster from Lincolnshire for our modern understanding.

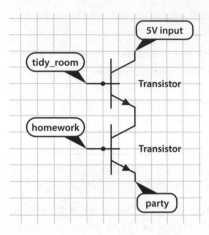

Figure 7.1: An AND logic gate made from two transistors.

The schoolmaster who classified thought

The phrase "party = tidy_room AND homework" would be easily recognised by George Boole (1815-1864) as a valid expression in what we now know as Boolean algebra. The young Boole was so obsessed with mathematics that he taught himself French so he could read mathematician Sylvestre François Lacroix's work in its original language. By the age of 16, Boole was teaching mathematics in a local school, and at 19 he opened his own school in his hometown of Lincoln.

Boole was mentored by Augustus De Morgan, who also tutored Ada Lovelace (see chapter 1). He took a professorship at Queen's College in Cork, Ireland and wrote more than 50 scientific papers in his lifetime. In 1855 he married Mary Everest, niece of George Everest, the surveyor and geographer after whom Mount Everest is named.

Mary Everest (1832-1916) had been a child prodigy. She spoke fluent French and longed to study mathematics at Cambridge, but the university didn't admit women until 1869 (and didn't award women degrees until 1948). Everest met Boole on a visit to Cork to see her uncle who taught Greek there, after which they corresponded avidly and eventually married. Their five daughters had distinguished careers in science and literature. After Boole's death, Mary Everest Boole continued his work, publishing *Philosophy and Fun of Algebra* in 1909, which explained algebra and logic to children.

Algebra of truth

Computer scientists are interested in just a few logical operations, usually AND, OR, NOT, NAND and XOR. A Boolean algebra expression is written with Boolean variables and a Boolean operator, and when evaluated it will return a Boolean result. Every operator's name explains what it does – for example, A OR B will evaluate to True if either A OR B is True.

We can explore more expressions using our parenting scenario. As Ada's parent, you come home from the country and the car is dirty. You know Ada hates tidying her room, so you give her the option of washing the car instead. But homework is still mandatory. So you change the party rule to:

> party = (tidy_room OR wash_car) AND homework

This will evaluate to True if either Ada tidies her room OR washes the car AND as well as one of those tasks, does her homework. Note that we put brackets around the OR clause, to make it clear that is evaluated first. Without this, by convention we would evaluate AND first, and Ada could get away without doing her homework as long as she tidied her room!

Boole's contributions to mathematical logic have many implications for computer science. We use Boolean expressions in selection and conditional iteration statements. For example:

```
if student = "Y" or senior = "Y" and fare > 5:
    discount = 0.1

if finished and total = 0 then
    print("no credit")

if day = 1 and not(holiday) then
    print("Go to work")

while not(found) and count < n do
    n = n + 1
```

And we can use Boolean operators in web searches, such as "cheddar AND cheese", to find only pages that contain both search terms.

Pause here and consider Fertile Question 3: "How is selection performed inside a computer?"

_____

_____

But this chapter is primarily concerned with Boolean logic in the design of computer circuits, and for this we owe much to the son of a judge and a schoolteacher born in Michigan in 1916.

Switch hitter

On graduating from the University of Michigan in 1936 with degrees in mathematics and engineering, Claude Shannon began graduate studies in electrical engineering at MIT. While there, Shannon analysed a massive machine called a Differential Analyzer, noticing that the relay switches that governed the machine's behaviour were always just on or off. This led him to recall Boole's work and suggest a digital "logic machine" that could not only calculate but perform "information processing". In 1938, he published "A symbolic analysis of relay and switching circuits" and the 10-page article is among the most important engineering papers ever written. By linking Boolean logic to electrical circuits, it opened the door to digital electronics.

Pause here and consider Fertile Question 4: "Why don't we use analogue computers anymore?"

_____

_____

Back to gates

A combination of several transistors which perform a logic operation such as AND is called a gate. We use symbols for logic gates to simplify our circuit diagrams, instead of drawing the transistor symbols each time. These logic diagrams are therefore an abstraction of the actual electronic circuit beneath, hiding the detail of individual components so we can more easily understand its operation.

So, when we want to solve a logic problem, such as **party = (tidy_room OR wash_ car) AND homework**, all we have to do is grab the necessary gates, set up the inputs of the logic circuit and read the output. Figure 7.2 shows the circuit needed.

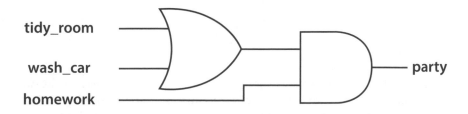

Figure 7.2: The Boolean logic circuit for "party = (tidy_room OR wash_car) AND homework".

We can see how logic gates can be used to perform logical operations with Boolean variables. But what about answering questions about numbers? Recall one of the high-level language selection statements from page 141: `if total = 0 then`. How can we perform this comparison using only logic gates? Well, checking equality to zero is easy, because NOT(0) = 1, so we just have to push each of the binary digits of the number through a NOT gate and then AND the results, which will be 1 if all the bits are zero.

Now what about comparing to other numbers? Well, we can decompose the problem `if day = 1 then`. into two separate problems:

1. subtract 1 from day
2. compare to zero.

We know how to compare to zero – we just did that. So all we need now is the ability to do simple arithmetic…

It all adds up

Binary arithmetic has only four rules:

$$0 + 0 = 0$$
$$0 + 1 = 1$$
$$1 + 1 = 0 \text{ carry } 1$$
$$1 + 1 + 1 = 1 \text{ carry } 1$$

Figure 7.3. The four rules of binary addition.

If we treat each single column as a logic operation, it has two inputs: each of the two bits we need to add and two bits of output (the sum and carry bits). We can show what happens with a truth table that has two inputs and two outputs, like this:

A	B	Sum	Carry
0	0	0	0
0	1	1	0
1	0	1	0
1	1	0	1

Figure 7.4. A truth table for binary addition. Sum and Carry are the two outputs.

We can now design a logic circuit that makes the above happen. The carry output is clearly just A AND B. The sum output needs to be 1 when either A is 1 and B is NOT 1, or vice versa. We can use two AND gates and two NOT gates to do this:

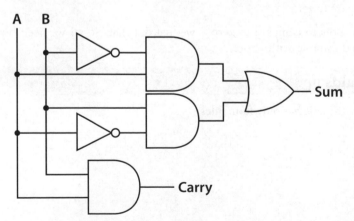

Figure 7.5. This circuit, called a "half-adder", can add two binary digits.

However, there is a special logic gate called "exclusive OR", written as XOR, that gives output 1 if either input A or B is 1, but not both.

XOR has a symbol that looks like the OR gate but with an extra line at the back. So we can use an XOR gate to tidy up our adder circuit, which now looks like this:

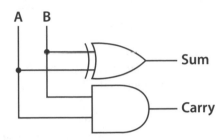

Figure 7.6. A "half-adder" using just two gates, XOR and AND.

From just two logic gates that perform simple Boolean operations on their inputs, we have an adding machine. All that remains is to string lots of these together and then we can add a big binary number.

Below zero

We can now add, but how do we subtract? Well, a – b is the same as a + (-b). Now all we need is to be able to turn a number negative! The first attempts to use negative numbers in a computer employed a "sign bit", a single digit to indicate positive or negative. But the logic circuit required to perform arithmetic with "sign and magnitude" numbers is complicated. Computer scientists realised that a number system called "two's complement" held the solution.

The odometer that records a car's mileage holds a finite number of digits. When run in reverse, it's disconnected to prevent unscrupulous car dealers running back the mileage. But if it did not disconnect, running a car backwards would subtract miles. Eventually the display would read zero and then the car would flip back to 999999 miles. Every mile driven in reverse would subtract another mile, so it would read 999998, 999997 and so on.

Odometer reading	Actual miles travelled
999997	−3
999998	−2

999999	−1
000000	0
000001	1
000002	2

Figure 7.7. A car's odometer run in reverse would flip back to 999999, meaning "−1 miles driven".

If we consider backwards to be negative miles, and forwards to be positive miles, figure 7.7 shows what the odometer readings mean: 999997 means a total distance of -3 miles has been driven. We would need a rule such as "A value over 500,000 means negative miles, 500,000 or below means positive", and we would have a way of representing negative numbers without a sign.

We use the same principle in two's-complement binary. As we count down from zero to minus 1, the digits flip from 0001 back to 1111, which represents minus 1.

Two's complement	Denary
1101	−3
1110	−2
1111	−1
0000	0
0001	1
0010	2

Figure 7.8. The four-bit binary number 1111 means "−1" in two's complement.

It turns out that these numbers behave beautifully when we perform addition using our logic gate adders above, hence the popularity of two's complement.

Go forth and...

So, we have addition and subtraction but what of multiplication and division? Well, multiplication is just repeated addition. For example, 3 x 4 is simply 4 + 4 + 4. We just need to repeatedly add 4 while counting up to three or, better still, counting down from 3 to zero. We have all the tools we need for this already: addition, subtraction and compare to zero. Likewise, division is just repeated subtraction: to perform 12 / 3 we just repeatedly subtract 3 from 12, counting the number of times we can do it until we reach zero. A few simple logic gates have given us the power to do really useful mathematics.

Pause here and consider Fertile Question 5: "How does a computer perform arithmetic?"

For a much fuller explanation of how computers work, I thoroughly recommend But *How Do It Know?* by J. Clark Scott[1] and *Code* by Charles Petzold.[2]

TL;DR

George Boole (1815-1864) published his paper "Mathematical analysis of logic" in 1847, describing what became known as Boolean algebra. Claude Shannon saw how Boole's work could be applied to electronics, publishing the article "A symbolic analysis of relay and switching circuits" in 1938. The first digital computers used fragile valves and slow relays. Transistor computers arrived in the 1950s, greatly improving speed and reliability.

Computers use a high voltage (around 5 volts) to represent either "True" or a binary "1", and a low voltage (close to zero volts) to represent "False" or a binary "0". A transistor acts like an electronic switch, turning the voltage on or off in another part of the circuit. Transistors can be combined into logic gates.

A logic gate is a collection of microscopic transistors that perform a Boolean logic operation such as AND, OR and NOT. Logic gates are combined into circuits inside a computer to perform arithmetic and logical operations.

ACT ideas for logic

Question It – second attempt!

Consider these questions again, then check against my answers at httcs.online/learn-logic.

1. Why do computers use binary?

2. What's inside the ALU?
3. How is selection performed inside a computer?
4. Why don't we use analogue computers anymore?
5. How does a computer perform arithmetic?

ACT key skill: summarising

Transforming knowledge from one form to another – such as summarising, distilling or reframing facts as questions – is a very powerful learning skill. When you summarise, your conscious mind must process all the knowledge and make sense of it in order to produce a shorter version of the same content. This ensures you understand it and makes more links in long-term memory so you will recall the content better.

I have done this once in each chapter, as I have written a "TL;DR" version of the content.

✅ Why not take my TL;DR section for this chapter and summarise further? Distil the content into a single paragraph, then a single sentence. Then pull out the three words that best represent this chapter. Finally, is there a single word that is more important than the others? Distil away!

Stretch It

✅ Why not find out more about half-adders and full-adders, and use an online logic circuit design program such as logic.ly to implement them?

✅ Likewise, you could explore the A-level concept of flip-flops to understand how the clock works to synchronise the operations of a computer. Some excellent videos to get you started are available from Craig 'n' Dave at link.httcs.online/cndboolean.

✅ Try writing truths about real-world situations, turning them into Boolean expressions, then drawing circuits and truth tables for them. For example:

- Yusuf will have a party on his birthday if he passes his exams and is not sick that day.
- You can ride the subway half-price if you're a student, but only on weekdays.
- Next year will be a leap year if it is divisible by 4, but not also divisible by 100.

Mark Mills has more of these examples and other activities on his website The Computing Café here link.httcs.online/cafeboolean.

Relate It

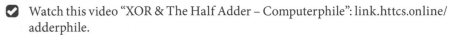

Although GCSE-level study does not require understanding of two-output circuits, the half-adder can really explain why it's important to study logic gates.

✅ Watch this video "XOR & The Half Adder – Computerphile": link.httcs.online/adderphile.

Link It

Link to programming

✅ For the sentences in the "higher-order thinking" section, you could also write Boolean expressions in various programming languages to understand the relationship between programming selection and the Boolean logic operated by the ALU. For example:

```
if passed = True and not(sick):
        print("party on Yusuf!")
```

Note that the expression "passed = True" could be simplified to "passed".

Link to networks

✅ Boolean operators can be used in web searches to improve the quality of search results. Try out Boolean expressions in searches and check the number of web pages returned.

Link to maths

Boolean expressions can be illustrated with Venn diagrams.

✅ Try this tool from Edinburgh University to generate Venns from expressions at link.httcs.online/vennmaker.

Unplug It

The 2008 Royal Institution Christmas Lecture series included an unplugged exercise where children acted as logic gates, and offered a video showing how to make logic gates out of dominoes at link.httcs.online/rilogic.

✅ Watch the video now and re-enact it in your classroom!

Build It

☑ The micro:bit can be used to explore Boolean logic. For example, you could code a program that displays different symbols depending on whether one or two buttons are pressed. See httcs.online for sample code.

☑ If you have a Raspberry Pi running Minecraft, you can make logic gates out of a special block called Redstone. Various tutorials for this are available e.g. link. httcs.online/minelogic.

I am lucky enough to have a class set of Unilab Decisions boards, which were made in the 1980s to teach circuit design. You can still pick them up on auction sites and they are excellent for getting hands-on with logic gates.

☑ Ask your teacher if you can get hold of a Unilab Decisions board and use it in class or an after school club.

Figure 7.9: The Unilab Decisions module, part of a discontinued series of teaching equipment but still circulating on auction sites.

Apply It

An after-school club is an excellent place to build actual logic circuits that you have designed yourself, if you can persuade your teacher to run one. A real stretch would be designing an ALU; a tutorial is available on the All About Circuits website: link.httcs.online/buildalu.

☑ You could collaborate on a website to explain logic gates to younger children, using glitch.com or even Scratch.

Correct It

Misconception	Reality
NOT is a binary operator, taking two inputs – for example, we see the expression A NOT B	NOT is a unary operator – it takes only one argument – so A NOT B is invalid. NOT B is valid, as is A AND NOT B. Remind learners that NOT simply inverts the input, 0 → 1 and 1 → 0. It therefore takes only one input. Some websites make this mistake, so if learners find A NOT B online, explain it is an error.
Computers understand binary	Computers merely process electrical signals using logic gates. Careful arrangement of these gates allows binary numbers to be manipulated. This misconception can be caused by early explanations of how computers work that include use of the phrase "computers don't understand words, they only understand binary".
AND/OR confusion	AND requires both inputs to be 1 for the output to be 1. OR requires only one input to be 1 for output to be 1. Confusion between two-input logic gates can be averted by engaging in plenty of discussion of Boolean expressions. Using the words AND and OR expressively helps, such as: The AND gate requires inputs a **and** b to be True for the output to be True. The OR gate requires either A **or** B to be True for the output to be True. NB: in GCSE and A-level studies we discuss two-input logic gates only, but chips containing gates with 3, 4 and 8 inputs are available.

Check It: Logic

Concept	Need to learn 😞	Getting there 😐	Mastered 😊
I know how logic gates work and can describe their role in the function of a computer.			
I can recognise the symbol for logic gate AND, and draw its truth table.			
I can recognise the symbol for logic gate OR, and draw its truth table.			
I can recognise the symbol for logic gate NOT, and draw its truth table.			
I can combine logic gates in logic circuits, up to two levels.			
I can draw a logic circuit from a Boolean expression and vice versa.			
I can construct a truth table with three inputs.			

Endnotes

1   Clark Scott, J. (2009) *But How Do It Know? The basic principles of computers for everyone*, John C Scott

2   Petzold, C. (2000) *Code: the hidden language of computer hardware and software*, Microsoft Press

CHAPTER 8. SYSTEM SOFTWARE

This chapter is about the software "glue" that holds a computer together, the programs that allow the applications to work with the hardware. We also take a look at the history of operating systems and utility programs. Did Microsoft really rip-off the Apple Mac GUI? Just where did Linux come from and why is it everywhere? Read on to find out...

Question It

First, take a moment to contemplate these questions.

1. Why do we need an Operating System?
2. Why did UNIX become so popular?
3. How can I run a game, browser and calculator all at once?
4. Why was Android such a runaway success?
5. We've had Command-line interfaces and GUIs, what's next?
6. How can I keep my computer running smoothly?

Again, you will be prompted to think about these fertile questions at relevant points within the deep dive, and you will get a second attempt at the end of the section.

Explore It

Palo Alto, California, 1982

Susan Kare is in her garage, welding a life-size steel sculpture of a razorback hog commissioned by an Arkansas museum. Kare has been a curator at the Fine Arts Museums of San Francisco since achieving her PhD from New York University, and she is happy to be creating again. "I'd go talk to artists in their studios for exhibitions," Kare would later recall, "but I really wanted to be sitting in my studio."[1]

She gets a phone call from an old school friend. Andy Hertzfeld is lead software architect for the Apple Macintosh operating system, and he shows Kare a rudimentary Mac, for which he wants some new GUI icons. Kare gets some graph paper and makes small images out of the squares and Hertzfeld transfers them onto the computer screen.

Kare joins Apple and creates some of the most memorable icons for the Mac, including the scissors, finger and paintbrush. Kare would later explain that her experience with needlepoint helped with the bitmap creation: "Bitmap graphics are like mosaics and needlepoint, if you like needlework, you'll love bitmap design!"[2]

As well as icons, Kare is tasked with developing fonts for Mac OS; she is determined to break away from monospaced fonts that make both a narrow "i" and a wide "m" the same width (a hangover from typewriter design). Kare designs proportional fonts, naming them after stops on the Philadelphia commuter train she had taken to school with Hertzfeld, including Overbrook, Merion and Rosemont.

Then Apple co-founder Steve Jobs stops by the software group. On hearing the font names, he advises: "they ought to be WORLD CLASS cities!"[3] So the Mac fonts become Chicago, New York, Geneva, London, San Francisco, Toronto and Venice. When the Mac launches in 1984, Kare's proportional fonts and simple but visually appealing icons help to make Mac OS the most user-friendly operating system on the market.

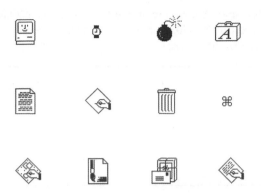

Figure 8.1: Susan Kare designed the original Macintosh icons on graph paper.

When early computer programs needed input or output, processing would halt while data was read from slow disks or tapes, leaving hugely expensive CPUs idle most of the time. The IBM 704 had a rudimentary batch operating system in 1956, but it just ran the next program when the previous one had finished: the CPU still sat idle while programs were waiting for input or output.

Battle of the North Atlantic

Two simultaneous projects 3,000 miles apart were tackling this problem. In 1956, IBM had promised the US Atomic Energy Commission (AEC) a supercomputer within four years. At 1.2 million instructions per second (MIPS) the Stretch computer fell short of AEC's target but was still easily the fastest machine on the planet when it was delivered to Los Alamos in May 1961.

Back in Manchester, Tom Kilburn fired up the Atlas supercomputer in December 1962, instantly doubling the UK's computing capacity. Atlas operated virtual memory, swapping programs between core store and magnetic drum, thus increasing the memory available for programs. ROM-stored procedures called "extracode" gave programmers built-in subroutines for the first time, including square root and logarithm functions. But the supervisor program was the greatest advance. Application programs would call the supervisor to read and write to peripherals, store data on the magnetic drum and handle overflow errors.

Both Atlas and Stretch's supervisor code provided multiprogramming features for the first time, switching between application programs to keep the CPU as busy as possible. A program was put on hold if it exceeded its time slot, or while a hardware operation was carried out.

Features of Stretch and Atlas were implemented in later OSs, such as IBM's commercially successful OS/360. Application programmers were now freed from writing code to perform hardware operations.

Pause here and consider Fertile Question 1: "Why do we need an Operating System?"

_____

_____

The 360-degree all-rounder

Stretch's best bits went into IBM's next big project, the System/360 – an undertaking so big and complex that it nearly broke IBM. But, according to the Institute of Electrical and Electronics Engineers' Spectrum magazine: "A short list of the most transformative products of the past century and a half would include the lightbulb, Ford's Model T and the IBM System/360."[4]

IBM's two flagship computers in the early 1960s ran incompatible software. IBM needed new standard hardware that ran everything and was upgradeable. To make it equally good at simple tabulating and complex mathematics, the machine needed an all-purpose operating system with more than a million lines of code. Sixty programmers grew to 1,000, the project overran by a year and the budget topped out at $5 billion, half the cost of the atomic bomb.

But on 7 April 1964, with some of the modules still in development, IBM president Thomas J. Watson Jr. made what he called "the most important product announcement in the company's history" and within a month IBM had 100,000 orders for the System/360. By 1971, annual sales topped $8 billion and by the mid-1970s IBM had 70% of the mainframe market.

The 360 operating system delivered features that are familiar to us today, including multiprogramming, a file system with indexed data files, program libraries, a job scheduler, interrupt handling and print spooling. OS/360 influenced the design of rival OSs, such as General Electric's Multics and Bell Labs' Unix.

With huge power...

At MIT in the mid-1960s, AT&T Bell Labs pulled out of the Multics project, frustrated by its complexity. Bell Labs researchers Ken Thompson and Dennis Ritchie embarked on a scaled-down version, initially calling it Unics, a pun on Multics.

Figure 8.2: Ken Thompson (seated) and Dennis Ritchie at a PDP-11 circa 1970.

The new operating system, now called Unix, was presented to the world at the 1973 Symposium on Operating Systems Principles, the same conference where, six years earlier, Larry Roberts had announced the ARPANET (see chapter 9). Unix proved hugely popular in academia, partly because of how powerful it was.

> "UNIX always presumes you know what you're doing. You're the human being, after all, and it is a mere operating system."
>
> Ellen Ullman, programmer and author, 1998[5]

When graduates were hired by rising technology companies, they often brought the operating system with them. Unix was written in C, so it was easy to port to other systems, and by the end of the 1980s Unix was everywhere.

Pause here and consider Fertile Question 2: "Why did UNIX become so popular?"

_____

_____

But there was a problem. Nobody was "in charge" of Unix, so many different standards and versions had emerged. In August 1991, an unknown student from Finland was about to change all that.

Penguins on everything

Linus Torvalds, a student at the University of Helsinki, wanted a Unix-like operating system for his IBM PC. MINIX was available, but it wasn't free and it couldn't be modified, so Torvalds wrote his own in 1991. A university administrator uploaded it to an FTP server under the name "Linux", and this name stuck. While choosing a mascot for the product in 1996, Torvalds visited a zoo in Australia where he was bitten by a penguin, and the mascot "Tux" was born. Open-source from the beginning, Linux took the world by storm and is now running everything from Google's web servers to Tivo set-top TV boxes.

"I get the biggest enjoyment from the random and unexpected places. Linux on cellphones or refrigerators, just because it's so not what I envisioned it. Or on supercomputers."

Linus Torvalds

Quick and dirty

In 1980, IBM needed an operating system for its new range of personal computers (PCs). When a deal with Digital Research fell through, IBM approached a small Seattle company called Microsoft, which was selling copies of its BASIC programming language on punched tape to hobbyists. Microsoft produced PC-DOS 1.0 in July 1981. IBM demanded that 300 bugs be fixed before accepting the software from Microsoft for $430,000. MS-DOS provided a command-line interface, like all OSs before it. But a small company based in Cupertino, Silicon Valley, had designs on a more user-friendly interface.

Pronounced 'gooey'

Steve Jobs and Steve Wozniak had co-founded Apple in 1976 to sell the Apple I personal computer, and a year later they had success with the Apple II. The 1983 Apple Lisa was much more technologically advanced but unreliable and with a whopping price tag of $9,999, Apple sold only 10,000 in three years. Undeterred, Jobs threw everything at the Macintosh, which became the first mass-produced computer with a GUI. Incorporating Susan Kare's visually appealing fonts and icons, and much more affordable at $2,495, the Mac was a huge hit, selling 70,000 in the first quarter of 1984.

For the first time, rather than typing commands at text prompts, users moved a mouse pointer to visually navigate folders, features and files represented by icons. The GUI model was adopted by most subsequent operating systems, most notably Windows, which launched in 1985. Initially, Jobs accused Microsoft CEO Bill Gates of ripping off his idea, but both parties had in fact seen the earlier Xerox PARC concept, and so agreed a licensing arrangement soon after.

Jobs quit Apple during a power struggle in 1985 and took several Apple staffers with him to NeXT Computer, which built the workstation on which Tim Berners-Lee hosted the world's first web server (see chapter 9). Jobs returned in 1997, when Apple bought NeXT for $427 million, bringing with him a Unix-based operating system called NeXTSTEP. Apple combined the look and feel of the classic Mac OS with the innovative features of NeXTSTEP to create Mac OS X.

Wow, it confirms DOS!

Apple had beaten Microsoft to the GUI punch with the Lisa and Mac, but Windows 1.0 wasn't far behind, launching in 1985.

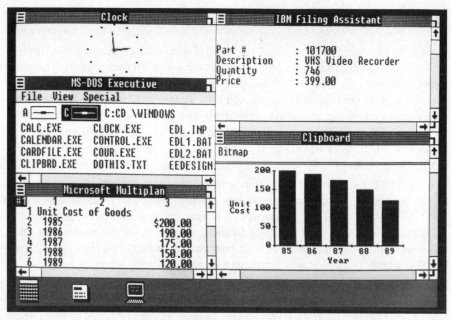

Figure 8.3: Windows 1.0 added GUI features to DOS in 1985 but didn't yet allow overlapping windows or true multitasking.

Little more than a GUI add-on for MS-DOS, version 1.0 had tiled windows plus a calculator, a calendar, the image editor Paint, a strategy game called Reversi, and a simple word-processor called Write. Although the user interface was very basic, even early versions of Windows included device drivers and cooperative multitasking, meaning it could run many programs at once, unlike DOS. Windows 3.1, released in 1993, shipped with support for peer-to-peer file sharing, virtual memory and TrueType fonts, at last allowing the OS to compete with Mac OS for desktop publishing customers.

Pause here and consider "Fertile Question 3: How can I run a game, browser and calculator all at once?"

Windows 95 brought full pre-emptive multitasking, meaning the scheduler could kick a long-running task off the CPU to allow others to run. The release included the Start menu and taskbar for the first time, the My Computer shortcut and the recycle bin, utilising a "desktop metaphor" interface borrowed from Mac OS. 95 also allowed long file names for the first time: previously every file had to fit the "8.3" format, leading to filenames like "alanscv.doc", "alanscv2.doc" and "newcvaln.doc"! Windows 95 started up with a short musical sequence composed by the music legend Brian Eno, ironically on an Apple Mac.[6]

Since Windows 95, the user interface has changed little, apart from an ill-judged redesign for Windows 8 that was reversed in Windows 10. Like Apple with iOS, Microsoft spun-off a portable version called Windows CE, which became Windows Phone. In 2015, to compete with Apple's Siri, Microsoft added the voice assistant Cortana based on a character from the popular Xbox game franchise Halo. Microsoft's Xbox games console runs a version of Windows, and in 2010 gained gesture support with the Kinect input devices.

Pinch me

The 2001 iPod used a simple embedded operating system. For Apple's 2007 iPhone, Steve Jobs was undecided on whether to build on the iPod's minimal software or shrink the Mac operating system to fit. Jobs ran an internal competition won by Scott Forstall's Mac team. It was a crucial decision, allowing Mac developers to produce software for the iPhone with little modification. iOS has a direct manipulation interface: objects on the screen can be tapped, pressed, dragged or pinched to cause intuitive effects. But, like macOS, Apple would not license its operating systems, so rival manufacturers had to look elsewhere.

Sweet sensations

A group of developers led by Andy Rubin founded Android Inc. in Palo Alto, California, in 2003 and created the Linux-based Android OS. Google bought the company in 2005 but kept the software open-source, believing this would encourage app developers to get on board. The famous Android logo was created by Irina Blok, a Silicon Valley designer who also did creative work for Yahoo, HP and Adobe.

Figure 8.4: Irina Blok, designer of the Android logo.

Everyone expected Google to answer the iPhone with a phone of its own, but instead it announced in 2007 the creation of the Open Handset Alliance of several manufacturers and mobile networks, precipitating an explosion of handsets running Android. Android version 1.0 launched for developers on 5 November 2007. Subsequent versions were named after items of confectionery: Cupcake, Donut, Eclair, Froyo, Gingerbread, Honeycomb, Ice Cream Sandwich, Jelly Bean, KitKat, Lollipop, Marshmallow, Nougat, Oreo and Pie.[7] (Sadly, Google have ended this tradition, leaving Android 10 without a sweet nickname).

Initially, Google's rivals were sceptical. Nokia said: "We don't see this as a threat." A member of Microsoft's Windows Mobile team stated: "I don't understand the impact that they are going to have."[8] But Android took 71% of the mobile OS market in 2021, compared with Apple's 27%. In 2013, Nokia abandoned its Symbian OS in favour of Windows Phone and later jumped again to Android; Microsoft ceased support for its Windows Phone OS in 2019. Analysts attributed Android's runaway success to the huge number of apps available thanks to its open-source licencing.

> Pause here and consider Fertile Question 4: "Why was Android such a runaway success?"
>
> _____
>
> _____

Amazon chose to "fork" (make a spin-off version of) Android for its Fire tablets, but with tight integration with its own cloud shopping and media stores, adding the Alexa voice assistant to its products beginning in 2014.

Type, click, wave or talk?

The first operating systems had a command-line interface (CLI): users would type commands at a cursor and the operating system would interpret and process them immediately. A typical Unix series of commands to create a directory and edit a file might look like this:

```
$ pwd
/Users/mraharrison/Desktop/docs
$ ls -F
data/   notes.txt   book/
$ mkdir essay
$ ls -F
data/   notes.txt   book/ essay/
$ cd essay
$ cat chapter1.txt
```

A CLI is powerful but not intuitive and novice users need a reference guide to hand at all times. If you know what you're doing, it can be hugely powerful but also highly dangerous: a single command can change or delete all your data. A CLI, of course, is far simpler to implement than a GUI and requires far less memory. MS-DOS ran happily in 64KB, while Windows 3.1 required at least 1MB. The more recent platforms, Windows 10 and Mac OS X, both require at least 4GB.

A GUI needs to keep track of all the pixels on a screen and redraw them when anything moves. Support for mouse, pointers, touchscreens, audio and video all adds up, and GUIs need more CPU cycles and more RAM, but the trade-off is a much more intuitive user experience suitable for the mass consumer market.

With the advent of Siri, Cortana, Google Assistant and Alexa, users have a new way of interacting with the computer – the voice command. Adoption has been rapid, with half of all internet searches voice-activated in 2020.[9] Voice user interfaces (VUIs) are accessible by disabled people who find traditional keyboard and mouse operation difficult. Gesture UIs are also here, with the Windows Kinect software development kit (SDK) allowing application developers to build gesture-activated apps.

Combined with predictive technology, this means the way we interact with our computers is set to change dramatically in the coming years.

> Pause here and consider Fertile Question 5: "We've had Command-line interfaces and GUIs, what's next?"
>
> _____
>
> _____

Computers in things

Most of the operating systems we're familiar with are general-purpose, multitasking OSs, able to run many different applications simultaneously. Meanwhile an embedded operating system performs a single purpose. We heard how the original iPod was built on a minimal operating system. If a device does only one thing, there's no point installing a hefty, general-purpose OS at great cost, size and power consumption. The Apollo Guidance Computer system (see chapter 3) is often considered the first embedded system: designed for a single purpose, responding to events in real time, and unable to run arbitrary programs.

Tuning up

Over time, a hard disk gets fragmented. Disk fragmentation happens because files are stored in chunks, usually 4KB in size, so when a file grows the OS grabs the next free 4KB chunk. Loading a file now causes excessive movement of the read/write head. A utility called a "defragger" puts the blocks back together, decreasing the file access time. Other utilities such as disk clean-up, backup, compression, encryption, antivirus and firewall are common system software, along with a selection of device drivers.

When an application needs input or output from a peripheral, it requests the operating system to handle the data transfer. The OS in turn talks to a device driver, a small program that "speaks the language" of the hardware device. The device manufacturer writes drivers for all popular operating systems. Both Windows 10 and macOS come with many popular drivers pre-installed and can download many more automatically. Linux tends to delegate this responsibility to the user, making it slightly less idiot-proof, but distributions such as Ubuntu come with Windows-level driver support that helps flatten the learning curve.

Pause here and consider Fertile Question 6: "How can I keep my computer running smoothly?"

TL;DR

Early computers were hardwired to perform a single program. Running a different program required extensive manual intervention. IBM created a simple operating system for the 704 in 1956 to speed-up batch processing, but a more ambitious IBM project called Stretch (1961) and Manchester's Atlas computer (1962) provided multiprogramming features for the first time, and abstracted hardware operation from the applications.

In 1964, IBM's OS/360 delivered indexed data files, program libraries, a job scheduler, interrupt handling and print spooling – the modern operating system was born. Two Bell Labs researchers, Ken Thompson and Dennis Ritchie, created Unix in 1971, which had become the most popular OS on the planet by 1980.

Apple's 1984 Macintosh was the world's first successful home computer with a graphical user interface, based on GUI prototypes seen by Steve Wozniak and Steve Jobs years earlier at Xerox PARC. Mac OS had a user-friendly interface navigated by a mouse. A year later, in 1985, Bill Gates's Microsoft released its first GUI, called Windows. Each subsequent version of Mac OS and Windows added more functionality, compatibility with additional hardware and accessibility features; mobile versions were spun off in the 21st century, including iOS and the Windows Phone OS.

The Finnish student Linus Torvalds released the first version of Linux in 1991, writing from scratch the features he most liked in Unix. Linux now runs hundreds of millions of devices from home internet routers to Amazon's data centre servers. Linux is open-source, meaning anyone can see, copy, amend and contribute to the source code.

Operating systems come in multitasking, distributed, embedded or real-time versions, with each type suited to a different use. OSs are a type of system software that exists to manage the hardware and to allow applications and users to interact with and control the system. Utilities and drivers are also system software: utilities help keep the computer running smoothly while drivers communicate with the hardware. Anything that is not an application is probably system software.

ACT ideas for system software

Question It – second attempt!

Answer these now that you have read the content, then check against my answers at httcs.online/learn-sys.

1. Why do we need an Operating System?
2. Why did UNIX become so popular?
3. How can I run a game, browser and calculator all at once?
4. Why was Android such a runaway success?
5. We've had Command-line interfaces and GUIs, what's next?
6. How can I keep my computer running smoothly?

ACT key skill: retrieval practice

As well as multiple-choice quizzing with Quizlet and Smartrevise, it's worth going a bit deeper from time to time by writing full sentences or paragraphs on topics you have learned. Don't forget to retrieve knowledge from topics you studied recently and not so recently: research shows that interleaving topics has the biggest effect on memorisation.

☑ So why not try a "brain dump" of all the knowledge you can recall about operating systems? Set yourself a Pomodoro timer (see Introduction) and write out an explanation of the operating system: what it is, what it does, some examples and where they are popular, what features they contain and how those features work. At the end of the timer, refer back to the textbook or a decent website like Isaac Computer Science, and check your answer. Write in anything you missed out. Then – and this is the crucial bit – do the same again two weeks later and see how you have improved. Rinse and repeat for best results!

Stretch It

System software use in context

✅ Try to list all the interactions between an application and the system software when using a computer to perform a task. For example: writing, saving and printing a Word document on Windows.

Task	System software response
Click Start icon	The mouse driver sets an interrupt flag to say there is a click event. The process scheduler puts one of the running processes on hold and executes the Interrupt Service Routine (ISR) for a mouse click. The ISR checks the location of the pointer, finds it is on the Start icon and so calls the GUI routine to display the Start menu, then returns control to the previously running process.
Click Word shortcut on Start menu	As before, for the mouse click. Then the OS finds the Word executable program in the file system, locates it on the hard drive, asks the hard disk driver to bring back the data, loads it into RAM and executes it.
Write content	The keyboard driver sets an interrupt flag for every keypress. The ISR for a keypress sends the data in the keyboard buffer to the current foreground application, which is Word. Word inserts those characters into the document at the cursor and then sets an interrupt flag to refresh the display. Display driver refreshes the display.
Save file	Word makes a request to the file manager to open the file directory. The user types a filename, the file manager checks this is valid and not a duplicate, then saves the file to disk. The hard disk driver writes the actual binary codes to the disk.

Once you've tried, check against my suggested answer at httcs.online/sys. Did you catch them all? Repeat this exercise with other common tasks, like playing a game or bitcoin mining.

Comparing Atlas to modern systems

✅ Research the Atlas computer supervisor program described earlier in this chapter and compare the features to a modern operating system. What is the same? What is different? What is missing? Tom Kilburn's 1962 paper describing the Atlas supervisor is available online at link.httcs.online/atlas.

Exploring human-computer interaction

OS user interfaces vary greatly in their usability and power. Modern OSs are designed using a branch of computer science known as human-computer interaction (HCI).

✅ Your job is to research the 13 principles of HCI, as described by Christopher

Wickens et al., and decide which are best met by which OSs. Start here: link. httcs.online/hci.

Relate It

Pizza metaphor for OS role

Various food metaphors suggest themselves for the relationship between applications, the OS and the hardware – for example, the pizza. Using the pizza analogy, the hardware is the base, the OS the sauce and the applications the toppings.

☑ Can you think of another food analogy that works? Draw a picture to explain the analogy.

Queueing metaphors for process scheduling

The scheduler can be compared to ordering fast food at a drive-through restaurant. Fast-food outlets serve meals fairly quickly to a single queue of drivers. But if a driver requests something that is made to order, they wait in a marked bay while the drivers behind are served. These bays are a holding queue for slower, bespoke orders, allowing the main queue to be processed quickly. This resembles a scheduler that places jobs on a low-priority queue if they request slow hardware resources, allowing jobs that require only CPU time to continue.

☑ Can you explain scheduling to a friend, using this analogy?

Hands-on with Linux in the browser

Experiencing different operating systems aids understanding of the topic and can dispel some misconceptions, such as confusion between applications, OSs and manufacturers (see the misconceptions table at the end of this chapter). The Raspberry Pi offers one way of doing this, with many operating systems available for free download.

☑ The website distrotest.net allows you to try many flavours of Linux, plus others such as FreeDOS, for that 1990s experience. You can try basic Linux commands in the browser at masswerk.at/jsuix, where you will also find a Commodore PET emulator and the world's first video game, Spacewar! More operating system emulators and other useful links can be found at httcs.online/sys.

Exploring Android versions

Alan O'Donohoe of exa.foundation has made a 15-minute video exploring the "Android Playground" at Google's HQ here: link.httcs.online/exapedition.

Link It

System software is closely linked to the topics of application software, translators, programming, networks and architecture.

Link to architecture, system software, languages and more

Designing a computer for a purpose draws on your knowledge of architecture, memory, storage, system software and more. Try the following task.

☑ Design a computer for each of these users. Choose a form factor, CPU, RAM, secondary storage, operating system, application software and network connection.

- School student studying for GCSEs.
- Games developer working in the office.
- Web designer who travels a lot for work.
- A self-driving car's onboard computer.
- A cloud service provider's web servers.
- A lawyer working in a home office.
- The check-in kiosk in a clinic waiting room.

See httcs.online/sys for suggested answers.

Link to networks

The speed at which we can transfer files over a network (see chapter 9) depends on the bandwidth and the file size. We can transfer files more quickly by using compression – for example, by uploading them to cloud storage or a file-sharing site.

☑ If the network allows and your teacher is happy, try copying a large file from one network location to another, or uploading to a cloud service. Then compress the file and check the transfer time again.

Discuss what has happened and how this relates to using cloud storage and streaming services. Windows and macOS both come with the ZIP utility, but you might explore the different compression utilities available as open-source or freeware sites, such as sourceforge.net.

Links to design

☑ Look back at the first Apple Macintosh icons designed by Susan Kare. Discuss with your peers how the Mac's GUI interface revolutionised the home computer. Consider these questions:

- Why is a GUI necessary for widespread adoption of an OS?

- What features of macOS and Windows make these operating systems popular?

Think of several stakeholders, including older people, disabled people and young children. Consider what makes a GUI important to them.

✅ Using graph paper or a website such as makepixelart.com or piskelapp.com, design icons for new features or apps. Try designing meaningful black and white icons in just a 16 x 16 grid, as Susan Kare did. How hard is it to make an icon that gets a message across in just 256 pixels?

You should appreciate the importance of user interface (UI) design and also how a very restrictive design brief can drive innovation.

Unplug It

✅ The roles of some of the features of system software are ripe for acting out in an unplugged activity. The process scheduler, memory manager and disk defragmenter can all be acted out using a little preparation. Discuss with your teacher!

Build It

The Raspberry Pi offers an affordable means of experiencing a Linux-based OS.

✅ If you have one you can experiment with the standard Raspbian interface, which offers a Windows-like GUI, as well as a command line interface with which to get to grips with the Linux file system. Alternatively, you can install the popular Ubuntu Linux, or turn the Pi into a single-purpose machine such as a Kodi entertainment centre or the RetroPie arcade (see raspberrypi.org/software).

Correct It

Misconception	Reality
Confusion between applications and utilities, e.g. "the word processor is a utility"	Word processors, spreadsheet programs and databases may be quite dull to some learners, but they are applications, not utilities. Learners should be clear that utilities keep the computer running smoothly, but beyond that they have no real-world usage.
Confusion between OS features and utilities, e.g. "the file manager is a utility"	File management is a feature of the operating system. The key features of an operating system include process scheduling, memory management, file management, I/O, a user interface and security. Utilities include defragmentation, encryption, backups and diagnostics.
OS is stored in ROM, or confusion of OS with BIOS	In desktop and laptop computers, the OS resides on secondary storage in modern computers. The BIOS is stored in ROM, and this includes instructions that cause the computer to load the OS from secondary storage. NB: mobile devices usually have their OS stored in flash memory, in an area known as the ROM, and this can be updated. Vendors usually upgrade the OS with an over-the-air software update.
Confusion between device manufacturer and OS, e.g. Samsung, Google and Apple all named as OSs	Android is an operating system published by Google. Google also manufactures phones. Samsung is a phone manufacturer that makes phones preloaded with the Android OS. Apple is a phone manufacturer that makes the iPhone, which runs the iOS operating system. Learners have experience of smartphones but sometimes confuse the manufacturer, the model, the brand or even the browser software.

Check It: System software

Concept	Need to learn 😞	Getting there 😐	Mastered 😊
I know the difference between applications and system software.			
I can describe the role of system software: to control the hardware of a computer system.			
I can describe the role of an operating system as an interface between the applications and the hardware.			
I can describe key operating system features:			
• Process scheduling			
• Memory management			
• File management			
• I/O			
• User interface			
• Security			
I can state the purpose of utility software and describe example utilities:			
• Defragmentation or file reorganisation			
• Encryption			
• Compression			
• Backups			
• Diagnostics			

Endnotes

1   Silberman, S. (2011) "Meet Susan Kare, the pioneer who created the Mac's original icons", *Fast Company*, link.httcs.online/karefastco

2   Campbell, O. (2018) "The story behind Susan Kare's iconic design work for Apple", The Work Behind the Work, link.httcs.online/kareicons

3   link.httcs.online/worldclass

4   Cortada, J. W. (2019) "Building the System/369 mainframe nearly destroyed IBM", *IEEE Spectrum*, link.httcs.online/ibm360

5   Ullman, E. (1998) "The dumbing-down of programming", *Salon*, link.httcs.online/ullman

6   Higgins, C. (2013) "Creating the Windows 95 startup sound", *Mental Floss*, link.httcs.online/95sound

7   Callaham, J. (2021) "The history of Android: the evolution of the biggest mobile OS in the world", *Android Authority*, link.httcs.online/androidversions

8   Popa, B. (2018) "Did you know? Microsoft, Apple and Nokia all mocked Android when it launched", *Softpedia News*, link.httcs.online/androidskeptics

9   Olson, C. (2016) "Just say it: the future of search is voice and personal digital assistants", *Campaign*, link.httcs.online/voice

CHAPTER 9. NETWORKS

This topic covers the history of connecting computers together, from the ARPANET that connected the first American universities, to the rise of the World Wide Web.

Question It

Now take a moment to contemplate these questions.

1. What drove the creation of the ARPANET (which later became the internet)?

2. Are protocols unique to computer science?

3. Is bad behaviour online a modern issue?

4. What key idea allowed the internet to expand rapidly?

5. What problem did Tim Berners-Lee try to solve by inventing the browser?

Again you will be prompted to think about these fertile questions at relevant points within the deep dive, and you will get a second attempt at the end of the section.

Explore It

Los Angeles, California, 29 October 1969

Student programmer Charley Kline sits nervously at a computer terminal at the University of California, Los Angeles (UCLA), supervised by Professor Leonard Kleinrock, and begins to type. Attached to his terminal is a Sigma 7 host computer, which Kline has been working on for a while now, but tonight is different. Network technicians at UCLA and at the Stanford Research Institute (SRI) have today finished installing the IMPs (interface message processors) establishing UCLA and SRI as nodes #1 and #2 on the Advanced Research Projects Agency Network, known as the ARPANET. Kline's job is to send the first message across the network.

It's 10.30pm. UCLA is ready to transmit, SRI is ready to receive, and Kline presses the first key. Just over 125 years earlier, when Samuel Morse had sent the first telegraphic message, the significance of the moment caused him to choose a biblical phrase. The message sent by Morse from Washington DC in 1844, which clacked out on paper tape in Baltimore, read "What hath God wrought?"

In 1969, however, Professor Kleinrock just wants to log on remotely to the machine at Stanford, so Kline is typing a rather more prosaic instruction: "login". But the universe has other ideas: the link fails after two letters are typed, and the first message transmitted across this new medium is once again suitably biblical. The first message ever sent over a wide-area network is simply "LO".

Pearl Harbor II

Kline's first "internet" message might never have happened had it not been for the Cold War. Twelve years before "lo" arrived in Stanford, the Soviet Union had won the race to launch the first satellite. Sputnik emitted short-wave radio pulses for three weeks in 1957 until its battery died, but the shock felt across the US was seismic. Americans were stunned, with some likening the moment to a second Pearl Harbor. President Dwight D. Eisenhower created the Advanced Research Projects Agency (ARPA) in 1958 to boost US technological innovation. ARPA's third director, Jack Ruina formed the Information Processing Techniques Office (IPTO) under the direction of Joseph Licklider. An expert in human-computer interaction and vice-president of technology company BBN (see box), Licklider initiated work on two vital technologies that would underpin the ARPANET: time-sharing and networking.

Bolt Beranek and Newman (BBN) occupies a special place in computing history, boasting several computing pioneers among its staff, including John McCarthy and Marvin Minsky, the "founding fathers" of artificial intelligence.

Originally specialising in acoustics, BBN was hired to analyse an audio recording of JFK's assassination, and the famous 18 missing minutes of the Nixon Watergate tapes. Modelling the acoustic properties of buildings and transport systems required lots of number-crunching, which drove BBN's computing innovations, including time-sharing and networking.

Lick's vision

Licklider, known as "Lick", had learned about time-sharing from the British computing pioneer Christopher Strachey, who had worked with Alan Turing at Cambridge. Strachey had patented time-sharing in 1959 for the UK's National Research Development Corporation (NRDC), and Licklider was determined to get it working in the US. Time-sharing allowed expensive computers at big universities to be shared between many users at once across a network. Computers were already joined up within buildings and across campuses. Such local area networks (LANs) existed in many US universities in the 1960s. But Licklider was thinking bigger:

"It seems reasonable to envision, for a time 10 or 15 years hence, a 'thinking center' that will incorporate the functions of present-day libraries together with anticipated advances in information storage and retrieval ... The picture readily enlarges itself into a network of such centers, connected to one another by wide-band communication lines and to individual users by leased-wire services. In such a system, the speed of the computers would be balanced, and the cost of the gigantic memories and the sophisticated programs would be divided by the number of users."[1]

Licklider set out his vision in a series of memos addressed to "Members and Affiliates of the Intergalactic Computer Network", which included his colleagues at BBN, plus many of the leading computer pioneers of the day at Stanford, MIT, UCLA and Berkeley. His imagination powered much of the early development of the ARPANET. Licklider saw the limitations of current networking technology and advanced a new technique called "store and forward packet switching".

Getting the message

Charley Kline's first ARPANET message travelled from UCLA to Stanford in "packets" of data, rather than a continuous signal. Traditional telephone lines are circuit-switched, requiring a complete electrical circuit from end to end. A circuit-switched connection can carry only one conversation at a time. If any part of the message is garbled, the whole thing must be resent. Breaking up data and sending it in chunks over a network, known as packet-switching, is more reliable and makes more efficient use of the network. Each node stores packets temporarily until they can be forwarded to the next node; the recipient rebuilds the message from the packets, and if any packet is missing that packet alone can be resent.

Packet switching was developed almost simultaneously by Paul Baran of RAND Corporation in the US and Donald Davies at the UK's National Physical Laboratory. Davies had earlier worked with Turing at the NPL on one of the first electronic computers, the Automatic Computing Engine (ACE). Davies' high profile helped popularise packet-switching, and the technique was written into the design of the ARPANET's IMPs.

It's good to talk

In late 1969, UCLA and SRI, together with the University of California, Santa Barbara, and the University of Utah, made up the only four permanent nodes on the ARPANET. Many other institutions were already keen to get connected, and fortunately the network's design principles allowed for rapid growth. The IMPs were independent of the host computers, handling network traffic on their behalf, so although some institutions ran DEC PDPs, others IBM 360s, and some SDS Sigma machines, this didn't matter – they could all talk to each other.

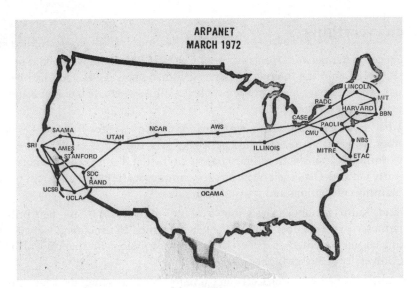

Figure 9.1: The ARPANET in 1972 had fewer than 40 nodes

With networking tasks abstracted from the computers into the IMPs, operating systems didn't have to change and the network could grow quickly. We take this "device-agnostic" principle for granted now: internet service providers (ISPs) don't ask you what technology you're running before sending you a router – the device will just work with your Windows desktop, your iPhone and your games console. In the 1960s, this was a ground-breaking idea that solved the problem of incompatible hardware. By 1973 there were 40 nodes across the US, and by 1981 there were more than 200 worldwide, including in Hawaii and London. IMP design was one reason for rapid growth. Another was the ARPA team's relentless focus on protocols, one of which was to establish the ARPANET's place in internet history.

Pause here and consider Fertile Question 1: "What drove the creation of the ARPANET (which later became the internet)?"

_____

_____

IP on everything

In 1973, computer network specialists Vint Cerf and Bob Kahn were about to turn the ARPANET into the internet – they just didn't know it yet. Cerf had been a graduate student under Leonard Kleinrock at UCLA, where he had met Kahn, an electrical engineer from BBN.

ARPA had now become DARPA, with the addition of a D for Defense. Research was progressing on packet-switched networks over radio and satellite, to enable better communications with military bases, aircraft and ships. Unfortunately, all these early networks had their own rules for communicating, with different packet sizes, naming conventions and transmission rates.

Cerf and Kahn set about designing a standard way for these networks to communicate. In September 1973, their newly formed International Networking Working Group presented a paper on the new transmission control protocol (TCP) at the University of Sussex in the UK.

In designing the new protocol, Cerf and Kahn followed the same "device-agnostic" principles underlying the IMP design, abstracting away the network protocols from the hardware. They believed that if they defined a set of rules for how devices should communicate, people could connect whatever hardware they wanted. If it spoke the same language, everything would work. With protocols but no centralised bureaucracy, Cerf guessed that the network would quickly grow organically. He was right.

The word "protocol" comes from the Greek prōtókollon, which literally means "the first sheet glued on to a manuscript". This sheet would describe the contents of the document, showing readers what was to come. The word came to English via French, where in the late 19th century it meant the ceremonial etiquette observed by the French head of state.

Pause here and consider Fertile Question 2: "Are protocols unique to computer science?"

_____

_____

In 1981, Cerf and Kahn published a series of documents describing a stack of protocols they called TCP/IP. This included TCP to manage the device-to-device connections, and the internet protocol (IP) to route packets around the network. On 1 January 1983, the ARPANET switched to Cerf's protocols and the internet was born. Competing protocols – different networking "languages" – fell away and TCP/IP won over the world.

Internet comes home

The day the ARPANET switched to Cerf and Kahn's internet protocol stack, 1 January 1983, is widely regarded as the birthday of the internet. By 1987 there were 10,000 nodes, mostly technology giants, universities and military institutions. But at the end of the decade, the first commercial services arrived on the internet and the number of users exploded. In 1989, for the first time, home users could connect their computers to the internet through internet service providers (ISPs) like CompuServe and MCI.

> Pause here and consider Fertile Question 3: "What key idea allowed the internet to expand rapidly?"
>
> _____
>
> _____

But the internet was full of text, shared over email, file servers and bulletin boards, because the World Wide Web was yet to be invented.

Mother of the internet

As computer networks grew, a new problem surfaced. Network devices need to be able to route packets to their destination efficiently. But a complex network might have lots of routes between sender and recipient, some of them circular, causing packets to fly around the network forever without reaching their destination. Another engineer at BBN, Radia Perlman, solved this problem with her spanning tree protocol, described in a 1985 paper with a poem she called *Algorhyme*.

I think that I shall never see
A graph more lovely than a tree.
A tree whose crucial property
Is loop-free connectivity.
A tree which must be sure to span
So packets can reach every LAN.
First the Root must be selected.
By ID it is elected.
Least cost paths from Root are traced.
In the tree these paths are placed.
A mesh is made by folks like me
Then bridges find a spanning tree.[2]

Perlman had worked with Seymour Papert in 1976 to create the Logo programming language, enabling children as young as three to program robots. She was inducted into the Internet Hall of Fame in 2014.

Remember your netiquette

The most popular service on the internet throughout the 1980s and early 1990s was an organised collection of discussion groups called Usenet, with hierarchical names that described their content, such as rec.arts.comics and soc.culture.usa. Topics that didn't fit into the main categories could be discussed under the anything-goes "alt" hierarchy, where you would find groups like *alt.startrek.vs.starwars* and, yes, adult content. Usenet at this time was a fairly benign, self-regulating community of students and academics, with well-established rules of engagement called "netiquette", but all that was about to change.

Eternal September

Every September, students arriving at universities across North America would discover Usenet and be drilled in "netiquette". In September 1993, however, an ISP called America Online (AOL) gave its many home subscribers access to Usenet. Users of AOL, CompuServe and many new cheap ISPs flooded Usenet, ignoring its "netiquette" social norms. A user called Dave Fischer, writing on *alt.folklore. computers* in January 1994, said: "September 1993 will go down in net history as the September that never ended."

Pause here and consider Fertile Question 4: "Is bad behaviour online a modern issue?"

_____

_____

You called it WWWhat now?

Text-based services such as Usenet, bulletin boards, file servers and email made up much of the useful content on the internet in the 1980s and early 1990s, before the invention of the World Wide Web. Home users needed a modem to dial an ISP, which was slow and expensive, so only computer hobbyists were online at home. The internet wasn't yet useful for everyone, not until a young British physics graduate made the next big leap.

In 1980, Tim Berners-Lee was working at CERN in Geneva, Switzerland, where scientists were collaborating on thousands of scientific papers at any one time and organising them was a struggle. Research meant jumping around between documents stored on lots of different servers, retrieving them one at a time using file transfer protocol (FTP). Berners-Lee had an idea: what if he could just click a word to open another document? He was familiar with hypertext, first imagined by Ted Nelson in 1963. Berners-Lee invented a coding language for it calling it hypertext markup language (HTML). He then created the first browser that could read and process HTML, which he called Enquire, initially for use only within CERN.

By 1989, CERN had become a huge internet node and Berners-Lee had another brainwave. What if HTML worked over the internet? Then CERN scientists could more easily collaborate with other academics around the world. Berners-Lee devised an application layer protocol for transmission of HTML, called the hypertext transfer protocol (HTTP). And he took his Enquire browser and made it better, calling it WorldWideWeb.

Figure 9.2: Sir Tim Berners-Lee at his workstation at CERN where he invented the World Wide Web.

This machine is a server

Berners-Lee also co-wrote, in the C programming language, the first web server software: HTTP Daemon, or *httpd* for short. In December 1990, he launched the first website – http://info.cern.ch – on a NeXT workstation complete with a sticker that said, "This machine is a server, DO NOT POWER IT DOWN!!"

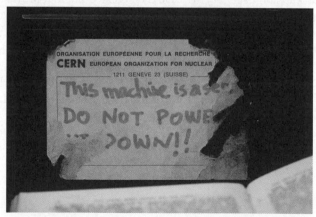

Figure 9.3: The first ever web server, complete with warning sticker.

Pause here and consider Fertile Question 5: "What problem did Tim Berners-Lee try to solve by inventing the browser?"

_____

_____

On 30 April 1993, CERN gave away the source code to the World Wide Web software. The user-friendly Mosaic browser was launched in the same year and by October 1993 there were more than 500 servers on the World Wide Web. Five years later, when Google was founded, that number had grown to 2.5 million. Today there are an estimated 2 billion websites, with at least 400 million regularly active.

TL;DR

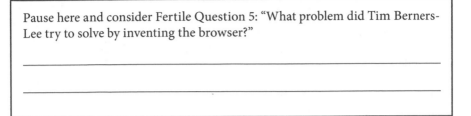

In this chapter we looked back at the creation of the internet and then the World Wide Web. We learned that in the 1960s, computers in university campuses like ULCA were joined together in a local area network (LAN). Then, in 1969, the first wide area network (WAN) was created between UCLA and Stanford, as part of the ARPANET project. This network was made possible by the design of interface message processors, known as IMPs, which can be considered the first routers because they joined two LANs together to make a WAN. The principle of abstraction can be seen in the ARPANET design: the IMPs take care of networking so the computers don't have to.

These early routers implemented packet switching, the process of breaking up data into chunks and routing it across a network, with the packets potentially taking different routes and being re-assembled at the other end. This is a key strength of the ARPANET, allowing it to grow quickly and perform reliably.

To make the newly networked computers useful, ARPA's visionary director in the early 1960s, Joseph Licklider, also drove development of time-sharing – the principle of allowing multiple programs to run on one computer, which is a key feature of all modern operating systems.

In 1983, the ARPANET adopted a set of standard protocols created by Vint Cerf, called TCP/IP. Protocols are rules that enable very different computers to communicate; the protocols are arranged in layers, with each layer performing a single job. At the top is the application layer, where email sits and, later, websites displayed by the browser. Throughout the 1980s, the internet was used mostly by universities and the military to access text-only services like email, FTP and Usenet. Home users arrived on the internet in the early 1990s thanks to the first commercial ISPs, including AOL and CompuServe.

Tim Berners-Lee invented HTML in the 1980s and combined this with TCP/IP to create the World Wide Web, which was made freely available in 1993. This technology allows a browser to download and display pages from a web server anywhere in the world. The web has grown rapidly and around 59% of the world's population is now online.

It's important to draw a clear distinction between the internet and the World Wide Web. The internet is a global network of cables, satellite links, switches and routers that join computers together. The web is the collection of websites, apps and services that make use of the internet to do useful things.

In the next chapter, we will look at some of the implications of the internet and the web, including threats such as SQL Injection and malware, and developments such as cloud computing.

ACT ideas for networks

Question It – second attempt!

Answer these now that you have read the content, then check against my answers at httcs.online/learn-net.

1. What drove the creation of the ARPANET (which later became the internet)?
2. Are protocols unique to computer science?
3. Is bad behaviour online a modern issue?
4. What key idea allowed the internet to expand rapidly?
5. What problem did Tim Berners-Lee try to solve by inventing the browser?

Relate It

The postal service protocol stack

To illustrate the concept of layered protocols, I draw an analogy with sending a birthday card to my mum. A typical postal service consists of multiple layers, like a computer network. The process begins with me writing Mum's address on the card. Then I put the card in the postbox and, later, the card drops through my mum's letterbox. This is the application layer of the postal protocol stack – it's the bit we see that is useful.

Similarly, when browsing the web, I type a web address into my browser application – Chrome, Edge, Firefox or Safari – and the page appears. I don't much care about what's happening in the lower layers of the stack; all I see is the application layer working and the web page being delivered by the HTTP protocol.

After I put the card in the postbox, my mum's birthday card is collected from the post office and taken to a local sorting office. We can call this the transport layer. Crucially, I don't care if this is done in a van, by bicycle, on foot, as long as this layer shuttles my card to the sorting office.

The mail is sorted, batched and driven in much bigger trucks to the sorting office nearest my mum. This could be called the network layer of the postal service and is another layer down in the postal protocol stack. Again, if these sorting offices move, merge or close, or if the trucks are replaced by trains or planes, I don't care. It only matters that the interface between layers – my mail moving from the transport layer to the network layer – remains intact.

From the sorting office, the post is pushed back up the protocol stack. It's sorted into batches for the postal delivery worker, who will take a bag of mail down my mum's street and pop my card through her door. Again, I don't care if the postman walks, cycles or drives; nor do I care which order the houses in Mum's street are visited. All of that can change and has undoubtedly changed over time. What's important is that this layer performs its core function, which is to regularly collect mail from the previous layer and deliver it. The layer continues to interface correctly with the layer above and the layer below.

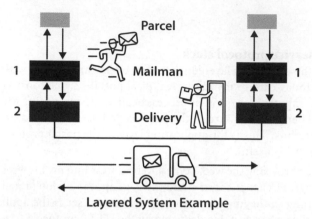

Layered System Example

Figure 9.4: The postal system is a good analogy for the internet protocol stack.

Post-it packet switching

To demonstrate packet switching, teachers often ask students to write messages on Post-it notes, one word per sheet, then add "To", "From" and "part x of y" on the top. They pass these notes from person to person until they reach the correct recipient. This demonstrates the principle of packet switching and its many benefits in a fun and memorable way.

☑ A detailed explanation of this activity can be found in the book *Hacking the Curriculum* (pages 59-62),[3] which you can ask your teacher to pick up!

Build It

Raspberry Pi web server

With a Raspberry Pi you can set up your own web server in the classroom, host a web page of your own making, and then connect to it from another Pi or any browser on the same network segment. This is a very powerful way of illustrating the principles of web hosting, DNS, HTML and HTTP. Full instructions are available on the Raspberry Pi projects site at link.httcs.online/piwebserver.

ACT key skill: glossaries, flashcards and knowledge organisers

We saw earlier how transforming knowledge helps us retain it more effectively. One way of doing this is by making a glossary of key words. This is a double-whammy approach, as the glossary can be used as a recall tool later, using the read-cover-say-check technique (see chapter 10).

✅ Read through this chapter and a decent textbook or online resource for computer networks (if you haven't got access to a paper or digital textbook you can use BBC Bitesize) and make a list of key terms related to networking. Write them out in a grid so you can choose to cover the term and guess it from the definition or the other way round.

✅ Alternatively write them out on flashcards which you can flip, and by doing this you can ask a friend or family member to test you on the definitions. Finally, you can make a "knowledge organiser" for the topic. Use your mind mapping, sketch-noting and glossary skills to make an attractive summary of the topic you can revise from.

Link It

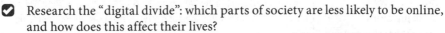

Link to issues: the digital divide

Fast internet is vital to modern life, providing access to education, jobs and government services.

✅ Research the "digital divide": which parts of society are less likely to be online, and how does this affect their lives?

Correct It

Misconception	Reality
Peer-to-peer networks are necessarily mesh or partial mesh topology, as shown in an image on this Wikipedia page: en.wikipedia.org/wiki/Peer-to-peer	Network service model (P2P or client server) is independent of the topology and star networks can be P2P, just as mesh networks can have a client-server model. The service model is an abstract concept, not related to physical connections, so using the same style of diagram for both topology and service model may lead to this confusion.
The server sits at the centre of a star network, as shown in an image on this Wikipedia page: en.wikipedia.org/wiki/Peer-to-peer	The device at the centre of a star network is a switch. The server is just another device on one of the "spokes" of the star. In the desire to illustrate an abstract concept, Wikipedia, like some textbooks, has embedded this misconception.
Internet = WWW, using the terms interchangeably or using the wrong term	The internet is a global network of networks, and the World Wide Web is the collection of websites, apps and services that uses the internet to do useful things.
Browser = search engine, such as using "Google" to mean the browser Google Chrome	The browser is a program that reads HTML and displays it on the screen. Edge, Firefox, Safari and Chrome are all browsers. Google means the Google search engine, or the company that runs it.
Internet access = Wi-Fi	Wi-Fi or wireless networking simply joins a device to a LAN via a WAP. The LAN may also have a shared internet connection, but not necessarily.
Google is the "front page" of the WWW, and all WWW usage must begin with a search	The "omnibox" interface of the most popular web browsers accepts either a URL or a search term. However, typing a well-formed URL will not cause a search to be performed and will instead open a connection to the website with that URL. But this omnibox approach has likely encouraged the misconception that all website requests begin with a search.
SMS and mobile calls use internet data	Texts via the Short Message Service (SMS) travel over standard cellular phone networks called Global System for Mobile Communications (GSM). SMS was launched in 1992. Internet Protocol (IP)-based messaging such as iMessage and WhatsApp came much later.

Misconception	Reality
Virtual networks provide secure remote access (confusion with Virtual Private Network or VPN)	A virtual network is a software network running over a hardware one. Network administrators often partition the physical network into virtual networks for security and performance reasons. Traffic that originates in one VLAN will not be visible from another VLAN even if they share physical hardware. For example, a university's physical LAN might be partitioned into student computers and staff computers, each in a different virtual network called a VLAN, despite all being attached to the same physical network. A business may divide its corporate LAN into separate VLANs for engineering, finance and HR. This is entirely different to a VPN, which creates an encrypted "tunnel" across the internet to provide secure access from a remote location to a managed network. VPNs are used by remote workers to access office LANs. The VPN is unrelated to the VLAN – they just share the word "virtual".

Check It: Networks

Concept	Need to learn 😞	Getting there 😐	Mastered 😊
I can describe a network as a set of connected computers and devices.			
I can describe network hardware components and how they work:			
• Hub			
• Switch			
• Router			
• Network interface card (NIC)			
• Wireless access point (WAP)			
I can describe different types of transmission media including:			
• Unshielded twisted pair (copper wires also known as ethernet cables or Cat 5, 6 and 7 cables)			
• Fibre-optic cables			
• Wireless network connections			
I can explain the characteristics of wired and wireless networking.			
I can explain IP address and MAC address.			
I can describe the types of network LAN, WAN and PAN.			
I can describe common network topologies:			
• Ring			
• Star			
• Bus			
• Mesh/partial mesh			
I can describe the relationship or service model of a network, which can be client-server or peer-to-peer, and the differences between them.			

Concept	Need to learn ☹	Getting there 😐	Mastered ☺
I can define the internet, the World Wide Web and the difference between them.			
I can define packet switching, circuit switching and the differences.			
I can explain the purpose of a protocol.			
I can describe common protocols and their uses:			
• HTTP, HTTPS			
• FTP			
• TCP			
• IP			
• DNS			
• SMTP			
• POP			
• IMAP			
I can describe the protocol stack and explain the notion of layers.			
I can identify factors affecting network performance.			
I can explain virtual networks and why they are useful.			
I know how to protect a network from threats.			

Endnotes

1   Licklider, J.C.R. (1960) "Man-computer Symbiosis", *IRE Transactions on Human Factors in Electronics*, HFE-1, 4-11, link.httcs.online/licklider

2   Perlman, R. (1985) "An algorithm for distributed computation of a spanning tree in an extended LAN", *Association for Computing Machinery*, link.httcs.online/perlman

3   Livingstone, I. and Saeed, S. (2017) *Hacking the Curriculum: creative computing and the power of play*, John Catt

CHAPTER 10. SECURITY

Keeping a computer system safe is the topic of this chapter, as we take a journey from the Caesar Cipher to the WannaCry trojan, and ask how we can protect against malicious activity.

Question It

First take a moment to contemplate these questions.

1. What came first, encryption or computer networks?
2. How important were computers in winning World War II?
3. Will quantum computers break traditional encryption, and is this a big issue?
4. Nobody can guess my password, so I'm safe from hackers, right?
5. If I've got antivirus software, why do I still need to patch software?
6. Developers should just get the system working, security features can be added later. True or false?

Again you will be prompted to think about these fertile questions at relevant points within the deep dive, and you will get a second attempt at the end of the section.

Explore It

Royal Institution Lecture Theatre, London, June 1903

An expectant audience watches the physicist John Ambrose Fleming tinkering with arcane apparatus. They are waiting for a demonstration of long-range wireless messaging developed by Fleming's employer, Guglielmo Marconi (now recognised as the inventor of radio).

Marconi is 300 miles away, preparing to send a signal to London from a clifftop station in Poldhu, Cornwall. Yet, a few minutes before the official demonstration begins, the apparatus starts tapping out a message. And it's clearly not from Marconi.

RATS RATS RATS RATS…

…types the Morse code printer, set up to decode the messages arriving from Cornwall. And then, even worse, the printer begins to tap out a rude rhyme about Marconi:

THERE WAS A YOUNG FELLOW OF ITALY, WHO DIDDLED THE PUBLIC QUITE PRETTILY…

The magician Nevil Maskelyne has hacked the demonstration; he has been hired as a spy by the Eastern Telegraph Company, a wired telegraph provider that fears the Marconi Company will push it out of business. "I can tune my instruments so that no other instrument that is not similarly tuned can tap my messages", Marconi had boasted just a few months earlier, and Maskelyne's job today is to disprove that claim.

Eastern had no trouble recruiting Maskelyne for the hack. The magician had previously used Morse code in "mind-reading" magic tricks to communicate with a stooge. After experimenting with wireless technology, Maskelyne had hoped to make further use of it, but he was frustrated by Marconi's broad patents.

Marconi doesn't respond to the hack, but a furious Fleming writes a letter to The Times, asking for assistance in finding the culprit. Maskelyne happily identifies himself, saying his prank was for the good of the public, since it revealed holes in the "secure" transmission. Maskelyne has arguably become the first "white hat" hacker in history.

Figure 10.1: The stage magician Nevil Maskelyne, who hacked a demonstration by the radio pioneer Guglielmo Marconi.

Eavesdropping

Maskelyne had earlier built a huge aerial and successfully intercepted radio signals from ships that used Marconi's lucrative ship-to-shore messaging system. His hacks revealed for the first time the insecurity of sending messages over distance and drove the adoption of encrypted messaging: scrambling a message so only the intended recipient can understand it. Encryption was used extensively on top of Morse code during both world wars.

Ciphers down the ages

The simplest encryption method is the substitution cipher: changing each letter for another letter or symbol. Julius Caesar is said to have shifted letters three places down the alphabet when sending messages of military importance. In cryptography, this technique is now known as a Caesar cipher. These messages could be broken at the time only by brute force: trying all possible keys until the words made sense.

Nine centuries later, a Persian scholar found a better solution. In Baghdad's House of Wisdom (see chapter 5), al-Khwārizmī (circa 780-850) worked on algebra and algorithms alongside Abu Yusuf Ya'qub ibn Ishaq Al-Kindi (circa 800-870), a philosopher known for translating and expanding on the works of Aristotle and Plato. In Al-Kindi's book on cryptography, *Risāla fī Istikhrāj al-Kutub al-Mu'ammāh* (literally "On Extracting Obscured Correspondence"), Al-Kindi described "frequency analysis" – cracking a cipher by counting how often symbols are used and comparing to typical usage in the original language.

When Mary, Queen of Scots, plotted in 1586 to assassinate her cousin, Queen Elizabeth I, she replaced letters and common words with symbols in her messages to her co-conspirator Anthony Babington (see figure 10.2). Sadly for Mary, Elizabeth's spymaster Francis Walsingham and his cryptanalyst (codebreaker) Thomas Phelippes knew about frequency analysis and were able to decipher the messages.

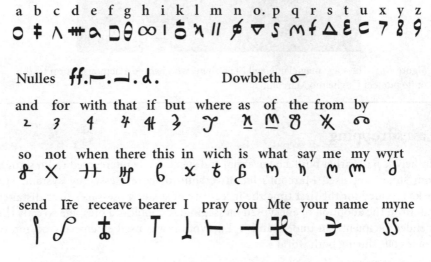

Figure 10.2: The substitution cipher used in the Babington Plot was easily broken by Queen Elizabeth I's spymaster

The decrypted messages and Babington's confession ensured a guilty verdict and Mary was executed in 1587.

> Pause here and consider Fertile Question 1: "What came first, encryption or computer networks?"

During the Crimean War (1853-56), Charles Babbage broke the Vigenère cipher, a code built on multiple Caesar ciphers that the French called "le chiffre indéchiffrable" (the indecipherable cipher), so during the First World War, a "crypto arms race" ensued.

Gilbert S. Vernam at Bell Labs invented the "one-time tape", in which a reel of paper tape of random letters was "added" to a plaintext message and a duplicate reel "subtracted" from the ciphertext by the receiver. This Vernam cipher, also known as a one-time pad, is unbreakable as long as keys are kept secret and not reused.

In practice, key tapes were regularly reused or simply intercepted. To solve this problem, machines with electric rotors to do the work of the paper tape were developed almost simultaneously by the US, the Netherlands and Germany. The best-known machine was Enigma, created by the German engineer Arthur Scherbius in 1918, a full 20 years before it played its famous role in the next major conflict.

The real imitation game

Early in the Second World War, German U-boats (submarines) were sinking so many merchant ships bringing supplies from North America that Churchill feared Britain would starve before the end of 1941. Thousands of mostly female codebreakers were working round the clock at the Government Code and Cipher School (GC&CS) at Bletchley Park in Buckinghamshire, codenamed Station X. To speed up this intelligence work, codenamed Ultra, the mathematical genius Alan Turing designed an electromechanical machine called the Bombe to crack the Enigma-encrypted German naval messages.

The enemy's ill-advised habit of including common phrases such as "weather forecast" and "Heil Hitler" in their messages often gave the British codebreakers a head start by gifting the codebreakers a short sequence of matching plaintext and ciphertext, which they called a crib. Turing's Bombe would test all the possible wheel combinations that matched the crib until further German words emerged and the wheel positions were known.[1] The Bombe (named after the earlier Polish Bomba) was able to crack Enigma messages in a matter of hours, allowing U-boats to be intercepted and protecting the shipping lanes.

Enigma was used by the German Navy, but from June 1941 the more complex Lorenz device was used exclusively by the German High Command. The head of the technological codebreaking section, Max Newman, enlisted the help of the electrical engineer Tommy Flowers to build a machine to crack Lorenz. His Mark 1 Colossus with its 1500 valves first ran in November 1943. Colossus could crack a Lorenz message in mere hours, which proved vital in the preparation of the D-Day landings in Normandy on 6 June 1944. Success required Hitler to believe the invasion was planned to take place hundreds of miles north-east at the Pas-de-Calais. A vast deception campaign of dummy tanks, decoy air strikes and disinformation passed by double agents proved successful.

A Colossus decrypt confirmed to the supreme Allied commander, Dwight D. Eisenhower, that Hitler wanted no additional troops sent to Normandy because he was convinced the Allies would not land there. On reading this on 5 June, Eisenhower reportedly said: "We go tomorrow." So convinced was Hitler that the Pas-de-Calais was the Allies' real target that he continued to believe the assault was a decoy invasion for several days after D-Day, refusing to send his elite Panzer tank divisions down to Normandy. As a result, the invasion was a success and turned the war decisively in the Allies' favour, although it took a further eleven months to defeat Hitler and completely liberate Europe from the Nazis. Some analysts believe the incredible efforts of the codebreakers shaved two years off the length of the war.

Figure 10.3: Servicewomen in the Women's Royal Naval Service, known as the Wrens, operating a Colossus Mark 2.

Pause here and consider Fertile Question 2: "How important were computers in winning the Second World War?"

_____

_____

Secret weapons

With computers becoming more powerful after the war, complex mathematical encryption became possible. The US adopted the Data Encryption Standard (DES) in 1976, which used a key that was 56 bits long. Brute-forcing DES would require trying 2^{56} keys which is over 72,000,000,000,000,000 combinations of bits. This sounds like a lot, but computers became powerful enough to crack DES in 1997, so it was replaced by the Advanced Encryption Standard (AES) which supports up to 256-bit keys. Both DES and AES are "symmetric" encryption algorithms: the same key is used for encryption and decryption, which relies on secure pre-sharing of the key.

Encryption without a pre-shared secret, known as "public-key cryptography" was unveiled by three computer scientists at MIT in 1977. Rivest, Shamir and Adelman's "RSA" is asymmetric, using one key for encryption and a different one for decryption. The "public key" can be shared openly, so anyone can send a private message without knowing a shared secret. Asymmetric encryption is slow, however, making it unsuitable for browsing and streaming.

When your browser connects to a secure web server using HTTPS (and you see the padlock appear next to the URL in your browser), a version of RSA called Diffie-Hellman key exchange is used to secretly create a random key known to both server and client; then the connection flips to AES using the now-shared secret key.

It's estimated that cracking an AES 128-bit key would take current computers 10^{18} years, which is millions of times the age of the universe. However, there are fears that quantum computing could successfully crack key-exchange mechanisms such as Diffie-Hellman within the next 20 years, which would cripple global communications, so the race is on to find the next big encryption advance.

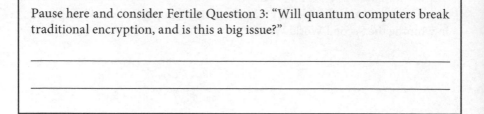

Pause here and consider Fertile Question 3: "Will quantum computers break traditional encryption, and is this a big issue?"

_____

_____

Phreaks and geeks

Before digital hacking, telephone networks were under attack. In the 1960s, the monopoly of the US phone company AT&T meant it could charge high fees for long-distance calls, so phone-hackers who helped people avoid these fees were applauded by their peers. Known as "phreakers" (from "phone", "free" and "freak") they made devices to generate the necessary 2600Hz tones played into the handset to get free calls. These "blue boxes" became popular on university campuses, and at the University of California, Berkeley, the top phreakers were the future founders of Apple: Steve Jobs and Steve Wozniak. Money from their blue box sales went towards buying more electronic components, with which the two Steves built their famous Apple I computer in 1976 (see chapter 6).

As the US telephone system was broken up and equipment upgraded, 2600Hz phreaking declined, but the phreaking community moved into computer hacking, trading tips on bulletin-board systems. When hackers stole passwords from naive new users of the domestic ISP America Online (AOL) by email in the mid-1990s, they called this "phishing"; they were "fishing" for gullible users but used "ph" as a nod to phreaking.

War games

In the classic 1983 "hacker almost starts nuclear war" movie WarGames, the eccentric professor responsible for the rogue defence computer uses his son's name as his password. The teenage hacker just has to do a little research about Professor Falken, try "joshua" and he is in. We're all familiar with the password. A password is "something you know" – one of the three basic factors of authentication. The other two are "something you have", like a mobile phone, and "something you are", like a fingerprint or retina pattern.

Combining two of these factors is called two-factor authentication (2FA) and it massively improves security, because a hacker might guess your password, but won't have your smartphone, and cannot fake your fingerprint or retina scan (yet!). (Google and Microsoft have gone with the phrase "2-step verification" just to confuse us all). Without 2FA, passwords – just like encryption keys – are vulnerable to brute-force attacks that try all possible values until one works. This is likely to be successful if the password is short or matches a dictionary word.

Pause here and consider Fertile Question 4: "Nobody can guess my password, so I'm safe from hackers, right?"

_____

_____

Repelling the wily hacker

"We keep hitting a damn firewall," exclaims one of the panicked engineers in WarGames who is trying to stop Falken's machine from launching missiles. The movie may have popularised the term "firewall", which originally referred to a barrier forming a fire break between two buildings. DEC sold the first commercial firewall in 1992. The AT&T network analysts William Cheswick and Steven Bellovin published the book *Firewalls and Internet Security: repelling the wily hacker* in 1994.[2] Firewalls are a vital tool for securing the network perimeter – the dividing line between the equipment you own and the public network. Since the early 21st century, Windows and macOS have both had built-in software firewalls.

Worms and viruses

On 2 November 1988, much of the burgeoning internet ground to a halt, infected with malicious software dubbed the Great Worm. The Worm's author, 22-year-old Robert Tappan Morris, was sentenced to 400 hours of community service and a $10,000 fine. Like all worms, Morris's malware replicated itself without human interaction, exploiting weaknesses in the operating system. It wasn't the first example of malware, but the first to cause extensive damage. John von Neumann had imagined worms and viruses back in the 1950s, and in the early 1970s Bob Thomas at BBN (see chapter 9) had created a proof of concept on the ARPANET called Creeper. Thomas's worm displayed the message "I'm the creeper; catch me if you can" before jumping to another computer and doing the same again.

```
I'M THE CREEPER : CATCH ME IF YOU CAN!
```

Figure 10.4: The Creeper worm was just a proof of concept, but it was so successful on ARPANET that another worm called Reaper was written to get rid of it.

Malware made the news when microcomputers became common in homes, schools and small businesses. A famous email trojan with the subject line "ILOVEYOU" spread widely in 2000. Hopeful recipients would download the attachment only to find it installed malware that stole passwords before emailing itself to everyone in your address book. The ILOVEYOU trojan, which of course the media dubbed "the love bug", infected an estimated 45 million computers worldwide.

Email worms known as Klez (2001), Sobig (2003) and Mydoom (2004) are still out there replicating. These worms were written to rope computers into a "botnet" – thousands of malware-infected devices turned into zombies under the control of a "botmaster" – for launching distributed denial-of-service (DDoS) attacks or sending spam emails. Mydoom is still thought to be responsible for 1% of all phishing attacks, 18 years after its creation.[3]

In 2017, the WannaCry ransomware virus spread across 150 countries, including the UK, where it caused huge disruption to the National Health Service (NHS). Around 200,000 computers worldwide were infected, mostly those running out-of-date software such as Windows XP.

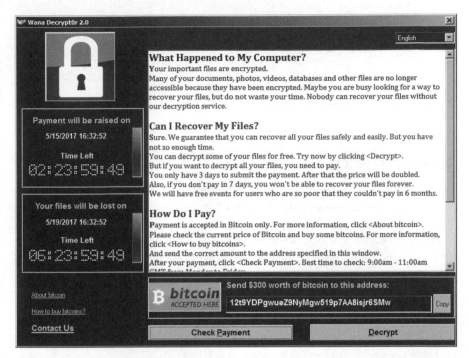

Figure 10.5: WannaCry ransomware ripped through NHS computers that were running obsolete or unpatched Windows operating systems.

These cyberattacks dramatically increased the necessity of cybersecurity, and in particular the need for spam filters, antivirus software and software updates.

Not everything is a virus

Malware comes in three main flavours. Viruses attach themselves to legitimate programs and replicate when launched by the user. Worms don't need interaction, they exploit features of the operating system to spread autonomously. Trojans disguise themselves as legitimate software or files, getting their name from the hollow wooden horse in which the Greeks concealed themselves in order to enter the city of Troy and win the Trojan War.

Antivirus programs work by looking for a pattern of bytes that identifies a virus, known as the "virus signature". But modern malware can mutate, changing its signature to avoid detection. This means antivirus is not enough: we need to prevent the malware arriving in the first place, and fix the vulnerabilities it could exploit.

> Pause here and consider Fertile Question 5: "If I've got antivirus software, why do I still need to patch software?"
>
> _____
>
> _____

Holes everywhere

The WannaCry ransomware trojan ripped through the NHS because many computers were still running the Windows XP operating system, or an unpatched Windows 7, for want of funding for upgrades. Any unpatched vulnerability can become a target for malware, so home users and IT managers must keep software up to date. But sometimes technical controls alone are not enough.

On 4 April 2013, a 34-year-old man walked into a branch of Barclays Bank in North London, posing as an IT technician, and connected a small device to a computer. The man was a member of an organised crime gang and the device, a keyboard video mouse (KVM) switch attached to a 3G router, gave the gang remote control of the computer. The bank lost £1.3 million before eight gang members were arrested and later sentenced to a total of 24 years in jail.

The gang had used a £10 electronic device and some simple social engineering techniques to pull off their heist. Posing as a legitimate member of staff is known as "blagging", "pretexting" or "impersonation", and the gang also conducted "phishing" and "vishing" (voice phishing) scams when they emailed and phoned account holders seeking their credit card PINs.

Social engineering exploits human traits such as the desire to conform, be helpful or gain social status. A strong network security policy and staff training are the best defences against social engineering attacks. The staff at Barclays should never have allowed "the IT guy" into the office: they should have checked his credentials and, if in doubt, called someone to verify his legitimacy. Staff vigilance against "tailgating" or "shoulder surfing" is important, as well as shredding all documents to prevent "dumpster diving". The Barclays hackers employed these tactics for profit.

Blocking the information highway

"Christmas ruined for millions" read the headlines on Boxing Day 2014, after a second day of disruption to the Xbox Live and Sony PlayStation Network (PSN) web servers. The hacking group Lizard Squad claimed responsibility for locking out millions of gamers on the day they wanted to try out their new gifts. Using a botnet, the hackers flooded the servers with traffic, preventing legitimate connections in a DDoS attack. A Finnish Lizard Squad hacker, Julius Kivimäki, told Sky News they had caused the chaos "to amuse ourselves". Kivimäki was convicted in July 2015 on more than 50,000 counts of computer crime and sentenced to probation.

Four years earlier, the so-called "hacktivist" group Anonymous launched a DDoS attack against Mastercard, Visa and PayPal in support of Julian Assange, founder of Wikileaks, whose accounts had been frozen. The attack in December 2010 prevented millions of individuals and small businesses from conducting legitimate transactions and cost PayPal alone $5.5 million. Four Anonymous members were convicted and two jailed for a total of 25 months.

DDoS is simple to perpetrate and difficult to defend against. Companies like Cloudflare make a living out of protecting web servers from DDoS attacks. They do this by placing their servers in front of the customer's web server, constantly dropping suspicious connections and blocking those IP addresses.

SQL Injection

Web servers can be knocked offline by DDoS, but the no.1 attack, according to the web security organisation OWASP, is SQL Injection. To understand how this works, we need to remember that all web forms have code behind them that makes them work; when I type in my password, some code processes the data I've entered. If that code is written badly, an attacker can craft some input that causes unexpected activity, such as querying the database or even deleting data.

SQL Injection can be easily defeated by checking input data for unexpected characters – for example, nobody should have quotes or semi-colons in their password – yet attacks remain common. Sony was the target again when a hacker group calling itself *Guardians of Peace* published unreleased movies and embarrassing emails from Sony Pictures executives in 2014 after a successful SQL Injection attack. We really must sanitise our inputs.

Bug-free by design?

The JavaScript that makes websites interactive is known as "browser-side code" because it runs in the browser. If a website does anything complex, however, it might run some code on the server instead; this is known as "server-side code" or "back-end code". If any of this code is poorly written, it could be exploited by hackers. That's why programmers often check each other's code for bugs during "code reviews", and why open-source software – with its source code visible to the whole world – is often considered more secure than proprietary code.

Pause here and consider Fertile Question 6: "Developers should just get the system working, security features can be added later. True or false?"

_____

_____

Protecting the CIA

Information security aims to protect the "CIA triad" of confidentiality, integrity and availability. Eavesdropping and data theft are attacks on **confidentiality**, damaging or changing data through malware or after an SQL Injection harms integrity, while DDoS reduces service **availability**. Attacks can be passive, meaning they change nothing (eavesdropping on the network traffic, for example), or active (malware and injection attacks). The key to keeping the bad guys out is to be aware of the "attack surface": the sum of all the ways, the "vectors", in which the bad guys can attack us. Just like bolting the door but leaving the windows open, it's no good having super-strong encryption, patching vulnerabilities every week and having security guards on the doors if 1% of your staff use the password "letmein".

TL;DR

Keeping secrets is as old as writing messages. Julius Caesar is said to have encrypted his messages by shifting each letter down the alphabet by a known shift key. The recipient would reverse the operation, only needing to know the key. An encryption method that changes each letter for another letter or symbol is called a substitution cipher; these are easily broken by frequency analysis, first documented by the Persian scholar Abu Yusuf Ya'qub ibn Ishaq Al-Kindi (circa 800-870).

More elaborate encryption methods were invented in the 20th century. During the Second World War, the Nazis used electromechanical machines called Enigma and Lorenz, which were cracked by expert mathematicians working with machines and early computers at the UK's Bletchley Park codebreaking centre. Modern encryption uses mathematical methods to ensure that computers cannot brute-force the key.

Before the internet, there was the telephone network. Students in the 1960s wishing to place free long-distance calls developed phone-hacking techniques called phreaking. The "ph" prefix persists today in terms like phishing (deceptive emails) and pharming (redirecting web requests to a malicious site).

Passwords are the most common means of authentication, but a weak password can easily be brute-forced by trying all possible combinations. Passwords can also be guessed or spotted while shoulder-surfing. A second layer of protection is added by two-factor authentication or 2FA. Typically, 2FA requires a code delivered by text message or a biometric indicator such as fingerprint or face recognition.

Attacks on the network include distributed denial-of-service (DDoS) and hacking attempts. Firewalls at the network perimeter will keep out unwanted network traffic, and websites should be fortified against SQL Injection attacks.

Malicious software rose to prominence in the 1990s. Malware consists of viruses, trojans and worms. Antivirus software can protect against malware, but other security measures such as patching software, firewalls and user training are vital.

Social engineering is often called "hacking the human" and includes phishing, pretexting and shoulder-surfing. For any company, educating users is important and this should be a part of the network security policy.

Finally, defensive design means designing systems to be secure in the first place. This can include secure network design, code reviews, testing and anticipating misuse.

ACT ideas for security

Question It – second attempt!

Answer these now that you have read the content then check against my suggested answers at httcs.online/learn-sec.

1. What came first, encryption or computer networks?
2. How important were computers in winning the Second World War?
3. Will quantum computers break traditional encryption, and is this a big issue?
4. Nobody can guess my password, so I'm safe from hackers, right?
5. If I've got antivirus software, why do I still need to patch software?
6. Developers should just get the system working, security features can be added later. True or false?

ACT key skill: read-cover-write-check

✅ It sounds simple, but all the best ideas are! Using a textbook, a page of your Cornell Notes, a knowledge organiser or glossary, read a paragraph or a definition, cover it up, write out what you remember, and check if you were correct. Repeat often for full effect! (Replace "write" with "say" for a quicker version, useful for last-minute exam revision).

Stretch It

Black hat or white hat
Security experts who break into computer systems are often described as either black-hat (malicious) or white-hat (ethical) hackers.

✅ Research these terms, then consider the following scenarios, deciding if the hacker would be described as a black or white hat and explain why.

- Lizard Squad's Christmas takedown of Sony PSN.
- The Anonymous attack on Mastercard, Visa and PayPal in defence of WikiLeaks.
- The Barclays KVM attack.
- Blue-box phone phreaking on campus by Steve Jobs.
- "*DVD Jon*", Jon Lech Johansen's cracking of DVD encryption.

Relate It

Exploring a real-life hacking example
✅ Research the real-life attacks mentioned above, and for each story, answer these questions:

- Why did they do it?
- How did they do it?
- What laws did they break?
- What were the impacts?
- How could we protect against these attacks?

Password strength checker
✅ The tech charity SWGfL has an excellent guide to password security at link. httcs.online/pwdguide. Read this and discuss with a peer what makes a good password, then try a few values with a password strength checker such as the one from the Open University at link.httcs.online/pwdcheckou.

Symmetric versus asymmetric
✅ 101computing.net has a great explainer for the two types of encryption, with an interactive tool for exploring them both, at link.httcs.online/101enc.

Trying out SQL Injection
✅ SQL Injection is more easily understood if you try it out – obviously on a demonstration website! One site where you can do this is hacksplaining.com.

Spot the phish
✅ You can test your ability to spot a phishing scam via the phishing tests run by Google at link.httcs.online/googlephish and OpenDNS at link.httcs.online/ophish.

Link It

Link to CT and programming
Encryption is an excellent topic to mix with computational thinking and programming. Writing a Caesar cipher is not difficult if you can code loops, but you may need help with the relationship between letters and numbers. In Python, the functions ord and chr swap between letters and their ASCII codes and back.

✅ Here is my sample code for a Caesar cipher, also available at httcs.online/sec.

```
plaintext=input("plaintext?").lower()   # input & make lowercase
shift = int(input("shift?"))             # input integer shift
ciphertext=""                            # initialise output
for letter in plaintext:                 # iterate over string
  pos = ord(letter)                      # get the ascii code
  newpos = pos + shift                   # add the shift to it
  if newpos > ord("z"):                  # if we go beyond z...
    newpos = newpos - 26                 # wrap by subtracting 26
  ciphertext = ciphertext + chr(newpos)  # append new character
print("ciphertext=",ciphertext)          # output the ciphertext
```

✅ Able coders will notice that this program does not validate its inputs and is written for positive shifts from 1 to 25 only. Why not fix these issues now?

✅ Another good cross-curricular coding challenge is writing a password strength checker. For example, it could check length, then count the instances of upper case, lower case and numerics and give a score. 101computing.net at link.httcs.online/pwd101 has an excellent tutorial.

Build It

If you have access to a Raspberry Pi connected to a network, then you could create a website vulnerable to SQL Injection that others can actually "hack".

✅ See the Raspberry Pi website via link.httcs.online/rpiweb for how to set up a web server on a Raspberry Pi and then the Guru99 website at link.httcs.online/sqliform for how to make a vulnerable web form.

Unplug It

✅ Decrypting coded messages is always popular, and I have included a couple in the Escape the Room activity on my blog at httcs.online/escape. Why not get your teacher to run this activity?

✅ Simon Johnson describes an excellent activity related to encryption in "idea 49" in his book *100 Ideas for Secondary Teachers: outstanding computing lessons*.[4] Learners must work together to decrypt a message, which turns out to be the password to unlock a laptop billed as a biological weapon! If your teacher has this book, ask if you can do idea 49 as a class!

Apply It

☑ Many competitions run each year that can be entered by teams of pupils, including CyberFirst Girls, Cyber Centurion, CyberDiscovery and more. Speak to your teacher about joining one of these competitions.

Correct It

Nothing gets a class exercised like the topic of network security. Admit it, someone in your class has once asked, "will you teach us how to hack, sir?" Unfortunately, because of an amateur interest in hacking, the classroom can be full of misconceptions.

Misconception	Reality
A DDoS attack steals data	DDoS is an attack on availability only; a web server is disabled so genuine users cannot connect to it. No data is stolen, changed or deleted.
Virus, worm and trojan confusion, or "everything is a virus" misconception	Because the term "computer virus" captured the public imagination decades ago, that term is usually used for all malware. It gave its name to the protection software – antivirus programs – although these programs defend against many types of software, including worms and trojans.
If your motives are good then hacking is acceptable	Often described as the "hackers' fallacy", learners may believe that probing a website's defences or attempting to guess a password is not actually unethical or illegal. They should know that just because something is possible, or no harm is intended, that doesn't make it right.
Confusion between penetration testing, vulnerability scanning and network forensics	Penetration testing is performed by an ethical hacker, who attempts to break into the system to determine weaknesses to be addressed. Vulnerability scanning means running an automated tool to check for missing software patches or other security holes. This is usually done regularly by the IT admin team. Network forensics is carried out during an attack and means analysing the data packets being transmitted on a network to identify where the hack comes from, how it is done and what data may have been stolen.

Misconception	Reality
The "padlock" declares a website is trustworthy	The padlock next to the address bar in a browser denotes that a secure connection has been established between the browser and the web server using HTTPS. This means only that traffic is secured end-to-end against passive attack (eavesdropping) by third parties. It says little about the trustworthiness of the website. Any web host can purchase a digital certificate, thus giving them a "padlock" symbol. Websites serving malware use HTTPS just as often as legitimate websites. The importance of the "padlock" has been historically over-emphasised, probably because 20 years ago HTTPS was rare and malicious websites didn't bother with it, so looking for the padlock was desirable. Teachers should explain the very narrow implications of the padlock symbol and advise that it is not a reliable indicator of trustworthiness.
Encryption prevents interception or reading of messages	Encryption merely prevents the understanding of messages. When using a wireless hotspot, for example, all the data packets are visible to anyone within range and a hacker could intercept these easily. However, if HTTPS is being used, the packets will be incomprehensible because the data is scrambled.
Encryption backdoors "for the good guys only" are possible	An encryption backdoor will be found and exploited by criminals if one is ever implemented. Encryption is vital for e-commerce and general privacy. Law enforcement has argued for backdoors – a supposedly easy way to decrypt messages known only to the police and intelligence agencies – to aid the fight against crime and terrorism. But technical experts agree that there can never be a "good-guys-only backdoor".
All ciphers are substitution ciphers	Modern encryption relies on complicated mathematical models that avoid simple substitution, which is easily broken by frequency analysis. The Caesar cipher is easy to explain and even to code. But it's important to discuss other ciphers so the learners have an appreciation of strong encryption.
Confusion between antivirus and firewall purposes	An antivirus program checks a file for virus signatures when it is downloaded or opened. A firewall will block suspicious traffic but will not check for viruses, so if a user legitimately downloads a malware-infected file then the firewall will allow this. But hopefully the antivirus software will detect it and prevent it from being opened.

Misconception	Reality
The Data Protection Act or GDPR criminalises hacking (confusion with Computer Misuse Act)	The Data Protection Act describes how personal data may be collected, used and stored. While it contains the principle that data must be kept securely, it makes no mention of hacking. The Computer Misuse Act describes the offences of hacking and virus distribution and associated penalties. Learners often confuse the many pieces of legislation. A number of scenario-based exercises, where they are asked "What law has been broken here?", can help.

Check It: Security

Concept	Need to learn 😞	Getting there 😐	Mastered 😊
I can define network security.			
I can describe common vulnerabilities in a networked computer system.			
I can describe common threats to networks such as:			
• Malware			
• Brute-force attacks			
• Denial of service attacks			
• Data interception and theft			
• SQL injection			
• Social Engineering			
I can describe common prevention methods including:			
• Penetration testing			
• Anti-malware			
• Firewalls			
• User access levels			
• Passwords			
• Encryption			
• Physical security			

Endnotes

1   Cox, D. (2014) "The Imitation Game: how Alan Turing played dumb to fool US intelligence", *The Guardian*, link.httcs.online/imitation

2   Cheswick, W. R. and Bellovin, S. M. (1994) *Firewalls and Internet Security: repelling the wily hacker*, Addison-Wesley

3   Gerencer, T. (2020) "The top ten worst computer viruses in history", HP, link.httcs. online/viruses

4   Johnson, S. (2021) *100 Ideas for Secondary Teachers: outstanding computing lessons*, Bloomsbury

CHAPTER 11. ISSUES AND IMPACTS

This topic covers the impacts of computer science on our world both positive and negative, such as the advances in medicine and the power of the internet to join communities together, and the issues of fake news, algorithmic bias and waste in the environment.

Question It

Now take a moment to contemplate these questions:

1. Is AI a force for good?
2. Are there any positives to being offline?
3. Can we trust the big tech companies to keep us safe?
4. How dangerous is "fake news"?
5. What is the environmental impact of a of a smartphone?
6. Why is the Investigatory Powers Act 2016 sometimes called the Snoopers' Charter?
7. How can we prevent algorithms from being racist or sexist?

Again you will be prompted to think about these fertile questions at relevant points within the deep dive, and you will get a second attempt at the end of the section.

Explore It

Beitar Illit, Israeli-occupied West Bank, October 2017

The Palestinian construction worker Halawim Halawi poses by his bulldozer for a selfie. After posting it on Facebook with the Arabic caption "يصبحهم" or "yusbihuhum", which means "good morning", Halawi heads off to work. He is oblivious to the danger he is in, caused by Facebook's AI software.

That afternoon, the police arrest Halawi and ask him "are you planning a vehicle attack with your bulldozer?". Facebook's auto-translate algorithm has rendered his caption as "attack them" in Hebrew. Halawi explains that his words simply meant "good morning" and, after consulting an Arabic speaker, the police let him go. Facebook has since apologised, saying: "Mistakes like these might happen from time to time." With so many dialects in use around the world, Arabic is considered particularly difficult for machine translation services.[1]

Racist algorithms

Several US police forces use an AI system called Correctional Offender Management Profiling for Alternative Sanctions (COMPAS) to predict the risk of an offender committing further crimes. A 2016 study showed that "black defendants were 77% more likely to be assigned higher risk scores than white defendants".[2]

A separate AI system called PredPol, used in California to predictively direct police resources to where crimes might take place, repeatedly sent officers into ethnic minority communities. The software learns from reports recorded by the police rather than actual crime rates, which researchers say creates a "feedback loop" that can make racial biases worse.[3]

In the UK, the human rights charity Liberty has criticised Durham Constabulary's use of a COMPAS-like AI system called the Harm Assessment Risk Tool (HART), which uses data on age, gender and postcode to predict whether a person is likely to commit a crime, as well as factors like "cramped houses" and "jobs with high turnover". As Liberty points out, "The predictive programs aren't neutral. They are trained by people and rely on existing police data, and so they reflect patterns of discrimination and further embed them into police practice."[4]

Pause here and consider Fertile Question 1: "Is AI a force for good?"

_____

_____

In June 2020 – amid worldwide fury at the murder of George Floyd, a 46-year-old black man, by a white police officer in Minneapolis – IBM, Amazon and Microsoft announced they would pause sales of their AI-powered face recognition technology to police in the US.[5] The algorithms misidentified dark-skinned women nearly 35% of the time, while nearly always getting it right for white men.[6] Alison Powell, a data ethicist in the UK explained: "Face-recognition systems have internal biases because they are primarily trained on libraries of white faces. They don't recognise black and brown faces well."[7]

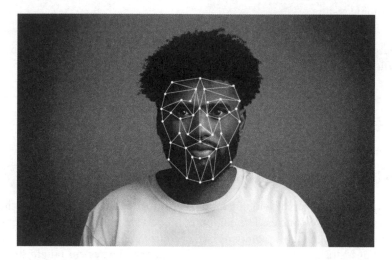

Figure 11.1: Big technology companies have paused sales of facial recognition software, citing the technology's potential for abuse or misuse.

Privacy

Even without face recognition, tech companies already know plenty about us. I downloaded my Google data recently and it came to more 2GB, not including tens of GB of photographs that I happily upload to the data giant because I like to backup and share my memories.

On Facebook I have another several GB of data, including family photos, groups and pages that I like, and a friends list. I'm happy to trade a piece of my privacy for the convenience of chatting with friends and colleagues, but I admit I came close to deleting my account in the wake of the Cambridge Analytica data scandal. Like many, I decided to stay for the convenience of sharing family pictures with my relatives and chatting with computing teachers in various groups.

To live in the modern world means to choose where to draw that dividing line between private and shared data; to choose which technology companies you trust and how much of your life you trust them with. As IBM puts it in a 2018 report, "Personal data is the new currency of the digital economy."[8] But all that personal data swilling around carries some risk, with more than 223,000 people in the UK reporting identity fraud to the fraud prevention organisation Cifas in 2019.[9] And as Halawim Halawi found out, where you draw that privacy line can sometimes have catastrophic results.

Pause here and consider Fertile Question 2: "Are there any positives to being offline?"

_____

_____

Old boys' (neural) network

In 2014, Amazon began developing an AI recruiting tool designed to select the best candidates for job vacancies. The computer models were trained on CVs (resumes) previously submitted to the company but, of course, most were from men. In effect, because of historic human bias in the tech industry, the system taught itself that male candidates were preferable! Amazon initially tried to correct for this bias but abandoned the project in 2018.

On 7 November 2019, the programmer David Heinemeier Hansson, creator of the Ruby on Rails web development software, complained on Twitter about gender bias in credit scoring by Apple. His sweary rant concluded: "Apple's black box algorithm thinks I deserve 20x the credit limit [my wife] does."[10] No laws had been broken, but Apple was ordered to improve the transparency of its credit scoring process.

One of Hansson's biggest frustrations was the company's inability to "look inside the black box" and explain the algorithm's decision. Increasingly, machine learning algorithms are spitting out results that their human operators cannot understand, much less explain, and humans are reluctant to overrule them. In her book *Algorithms of Oppression: how search engines reinforce racism*, Safiya Umoja Noble predicts that "artificial intelligence will become a major human rights issue in the twenty-first century".[11]

With great power...

Google performs 90% of the searches made from desktop computers. We trust the search giant to return what we're looking for 3.5 billion times per day[12] but, as the Swedish technology journalist Andreas Ekström explained in a 2015 TED talk, the results may be more biased than we think.[13]

In 2009, an image of the US first lady Michelle Obama with monkey features went viral. Google acted swiftly and the image dropped off the first page of search results. Two years later, Norway's worst ever terrorist attacks resulted in the tragic deaths of 77 people, many of whom were teenagers attending a summer camp. Determined that the murderer, a man named Anders Behring Breivik, would not gain the publicity he craved for his far-right manifesto, Swedish web developer Nikke Lindqvist told his followers to publish pictures of dog poop online with the filename file *breivik.jpeg*. Soon, if you googled "Breivik", images of dog poop would appear. And this time, crucially, Google did not intervene. Few people would criticise Google's conduct: most would judge Obama an honourable person and Breivik a despicable person. But is it right that Google gets to decide who's honourable and who's despicable, and not our elected representatives?

> Pause here and consider Fertile Question 3: "Can we trust the big tech companies to keep us safe?"
>
> _____
>
> _____

Autopilot overpromises

Biased search results may be described as censorship but are unlikely to be a life-or-death matter. Not so for high-tech carmaker Tesla. In March 2018, 38-year-old

Apple employee Walter Huang was playing "Three Kingdoms mobile edition" on his company-issued iPhone when his Tesla drove straight into a barrier. Huang later died of his injuries. His car was driving in Autopilot mode, which critics say should be renamed. As of March 2021, US regulators are investigating 23 separate accidents involving Tesla's driver-assist technology.

Inside the black box

New York City's Mount Sinai Hospital's Deep Patient software predicted diseases including cancer with exceptional accuracy. But it didn't explain its diagnoses, so doctors refused to change patients' prescriptions. Unable to see into the black box, the hospital declared the system useless.

So, if algorithms have all these problems why are they so popular? Because they often work spectacularly well. In 2016, a medical conference in Prague ran a competition to detect cancer cells. Harvard's deep-learning algorithm PathAI won with 92% accuracy, not far short of human accuracy of 96%. However, when the algorithm paired up with the doctors, performance rose to a staggering 99.5%.[14] The power of AI to look for patterns in images, medical records or DNA data is driving a revolution in healthcare, with spending on AI set to top $34 billion by 2025.[15]

Pause here and consider Fertile Question 1 again: "Is AI a force for good?"

_____

_____

The social dilemma

In 2012, Facebook added organ-donor status to profiles. Nearly 60,000 took advantage on the first day. Social host-finding site Couchsurfing was enabling low-budget travelling years before Airbnb made a billion-dollar business out of the idea. Social media is now routinely used around the world in the search for missing people. While social media can undoubtedly be a force for good, raising awareness of health campaigns, connecting divided people and amplifying the voice of the individual, its vast reach can also be exploited by governments and corporations in order to manipulate public opinion.

In the run-up to the UK's Brexit referendum on EU membership, the official Vote Leave campaign paid Facebook £2.7 million for targeted ads. The ads included emotive but fact-free claims including "The EU blocks our ability to speak out and protect polar bears!"[16] The ads were created by Aggregate AIQ, a Canadian company with links to Cambridge Analytica, the consulting firm that harvested private data from Facebook users.[17]

The QAnon conspiracy theory in the US, which began around 2017 on the imageboard 4chan, has swelled to hundreds of thousands of people who believe a completely unfounded narrative that Donald Trump is waging a secret war against elite Satan-worshipping paedophiles in government. Many QAnon followers came straight from the 2016 alt-right Pizzagate conspiracy theory, which falsely claimed there was a child sex ring operating from the basement of a pizzeria in Washington DC. Edgar Welch, a 28-year-old man from North Carolina, arrived at the pizzeria with a semi-automatic rifle and fired three shots in an attempt to "rescue" non-existent children.[18]

In 2019, the FBI issued a bulletin warning that conspiracy theory-driven domestic extremism was a growing threat.[19] The US Combating Terrorism Center has described QAnon as a "novel challenge to public security".[20] And when rioters stormed the US Capitol on 6 January 2021, in an effort to overturn Donald Trump's election defeat, all eyes turned to social media, where Trump supporters had been discussing the protest on QAnon-related pages for weeks.

Back in the UK, as Covid-19 spread during 2020, social media conspiracy theorists had a field day, blaming the virus on 5G mobile masts, calling it a deliberate attempt to control the world's population, and claiming the vaccine program was a secret plot to "chip" us all.[21] A "troll farm" in the Russian city of St Petersburg allegedly employs young people to spread misinformation and sow division using social media, with the intention of destabilising society in the US and Europe.[22]

Pause here and consider Fertile Question 4: "How dangerous is 'fake news'"?

_____

_____

Growing concerns over pornography, child abuse images, gambling, suicide promotion and extremist material have forced governments to act. The UK's online harms bill, still being debated at the time of writing, will give the communications regulator Ofcom sweeping powers to limit the spread of harmful content. Germany already has similar tough legislation, as does Australia. The world is beginning to see the internet as a quasi-public space where user safety must be paramount.

Energy

Elon Musk's Tesla very publicly bought $1.5 billion of the cryptocurrency bitcoin in February 2021. The decentralised currency – based on solving cryptographic problems whose solutions are rare – was launched in 2009 and has created many "bitcoin millionaires", with a single bitcoin rising in value from 30 cents in 2011 to $60,000 in 2021. But the computing power being used to "mine" the currency and add transactions to the blockchain now exceeds the energy consumption of Argentina.[23] Meanwhile, data centres are likely to gobble up 8% of the world's electricity by 2030.[24] And that new iPhone in your pocket? It has a carbon footprint of around 78kg of CO_2.[25]

Our rare earth

Energy is not the only environmental issue. The entire continent of Africa currently produces only about 2.9 million tonnes (Mt) of electronic waste annually, according to the UN[26], but Nigeria alone is the destination for more than 1 Mt of e-waste every year, much of which is imported illegally from North America and Europe. Once there, valuable metals are recovered in hazardous conditions, often by children with their bare hands, using furnaces and chemicals. And in 2012, Unicef estimated that 40,000 children were working in mines across the Democratic Republic of Congo, mostly digging cobalt for lithium batteries to power the 400 million new smartphones made each year.[27]

> Pause here and consider Fertile Question 5: "What is the environmental impact of a smartphone?"
>
> _____
>
> _____

Lawmakers and lawbreakers

Exporting e-waste to developing nations is actually illegal under the EU's Basel Convention on hazardous waste, but a two-year investigation revealed the practice was still widespread.[28]

Figure 11.2: Low-income Ghanaians endure harsh conditions to recover metal from electronic waste in the Agbogbloshie surbub of Accra.

The Waste Electrical and Electronic Equipment Regulations 2013 is among several important laws that govern the IT industry. The Computer Misuse Act 1990 criminalised hacking for the first time but the 30-year-old act has been criticised recently for preventing investigators from dealing effectively with online threats while overpunishing immature defendants.[29] US legislators are considering legalising "hack back" laws that allow companies to retaliate to online attacks.[30]

The UK's Data Protection Act 2018 brought data privacy laws up to date giving consumers and regulators more power. The Copyright, Designs and Patents Act 1988 gives creators of digital media the right to get paid for their work. Music, books, videos, games and software are all covered by copyright law. And the Investigatory Powers Act 2016 gives sweeping powers to UK security services. Critics dubbed the original bill a Snoopers' Charter for its broad expansion of police powers.

One thing everyone agrees on is that our vital computerised services need regulation, but there is obvious conflict between individual freedom and the common good.

Pause here and consider Fertile Question 6: "Why is the Investigatory Powers Act 2016 sometimes called the Snoopers' Charter?"

_____

_____

What now?

"The Fourth Industrial Revolution" was the theme of the 2016 World Economic Forum Annual Meeting in Davos, Switzerland. After steam, electricity and computers, our new age of mobile internet, automation and AI brings boundless possibilities but also unprecedented challenge. Computer scientists must work with legislators to ensure technology is a force for good. Algorithmic bias, harmful content, disinformation and radicalisation are huge challenges that need an informed, intelligent response. As Hannah Fry writes in her book Hello World:

"Perhaps the answer is to build algorithms to be contestable from the ground up. Imagine that we designed them to support humans in their decisions, rather than instruct them. To be transparent about why they came to a particular decision, rather than just inform us of the result."[31]

Pause here and consider Fertile Question 7: " How can we prevent algorithms from being racist or sexist?"

_____

_____

The tech magazine ZDNet has predicted the rise of AI-powered malware, which can learn how to get around our defences. "Low-code" app development platforms allow non-programmers to create apps.[32] Virtual reality, augmented reality and extended reality are set to become big, and the Internet of Things will reach 25 billion devices by 2030. But the field of AI is a growing cause for concern. In 2015, Stephen Hawking and Elon Musk put their signatures to an open letter warning that "the development of full artificial intelligence could spell the end of the human race" because AI would take off on its own, developing far beyond our own intelligence and resisting any attempts to stop it.[33]

In my recruitment speeches to students choosing their options in both Year 9 and Year 11, I encourage them to choose computer science and "join the fight against the robot apocalypse". Maybe that humorous challenge is not actually so far-fetched! Whether or not the robot apocalypse comes before we can solve climate change, it's clear that the world's major issues can either be worsened by technology or ultimately solved. It's our job as computer scientists to be part of the solution, not part of the problem.

TL;DR

Information technology caused a "third industrial revolution" and analysts are calling the convergence of mobile internet, automation and AI the "fourth industrial revolution". With all new technology comes both opportunities and challenges.

We face privacy, legal, cultural, environmental and ethical questions, and many issues span two or more of those categories, such as automation, spam and viruses. Most technology decisions require the balancing of competing issues and impacts – for example, automation drives down the cost of production and eliminates hazardous occupations, but can cut jobs or worsen inequality. The internet has opened up communications previously impossible, but has created a digital divide between those with access and those without.

Artificial intelligence is opening up huge possibilities in fields as diverse as healthcare, transport and the arts, but there are fears over bias, discrimination and lack of transparency. Cryptocurrencies such as bitcoin have been criticised for their energy use, and electronic waste is a growing ethical, environmental and legal issue, while finite resources needed in smartphones are mined by low-paid workers in exploitative practices.

In every question about issues and impacts of technology, we must consider all the stakeholders involved, including the creators, vendors, shareholders, consumers and wider society.

ACT ideas for issues and impacts

Question It – second attempt!

Answer these now that you have read the content and check your answers against mine at httcs.online/learn-issues.

1. Is AI a force for good?
2. Are there any positives to being offline?
3. Can we trust the big tech companies to keep us safe?
4. How dangerous is "fake news"?
5. What is the environmental impact of a of a smartphone?
6. Why is the Investigatory Powers Act 2016 sometimes called the Snoopers' Charter?
7. How can we prevent algorithms from being racist or sexist?

ACT key skill: revisiting Cornell notes

You will remember in chapter 1 we learned how to make Cornell notes and I asked you to write yourself a series of questions in the left-hand "cues" column.

✅ Go back to the "cues" for any topic now and answer one of the questions. When you do, tick it off on the notes so you know you have answered it once, and write another question related to the topic beneath it. Do this again in a few weeks. The key to effective use of Cornell notes is to keep revisiting them over and over to make the learning stick.

Stretch It

To develop your higher-order thinking skills, you could attempt the following tasks.

Legislation brain dump
✅ List all the ways that school computers are affected by legislation. After explaining the legislation, create a grid of aspects of the computer systems and the relevant laws. See httcs.online/issues for my example.

Gaps in legislation
✅ What gaps are there in legislation that need to be filled? For example, is it right that employers are able to trawl social media and fire people for comments they made many years ago? Does social media need better policing against hate

speech or radicalisation? Ask your teacher these questions or get a debate going with your classmates!

Relate It

List the issues

Consider one of the stories discussed in this chapter, such as the Palestinian construction worker who was implicated by poor automatic translation, or the mountain of e-waste illegally exported to developing nations each year.

- ☑ Discuss the privacy, legal, ethical, environmental and cultural implications of the role of technology in the story.

The moral machine

- ☑ Try the Moral Machine, developed by MIT (moralmachine.net) where you have to decide in varying scenarios, whether a self-driving car with brake failure should continue in its lane and hit a pedestrian or animal, or swerve into the other lane to hit a different pedestrian/animal. Each decision requires the learner to make a value judgement about who/what to save.

- ☑ Have a go, then discuss the ethics of self-driving cars. You could consider these questions:

  - Should a self-driving car protect its occupants at all costs?
  - Should the human pilot always be responsible for a self-driving car?
  - What legislation would be appropriate to reduce the potential harm of self-driving cars?
  - In 20 years' time, will we consider human drivers more dangerous than AI drivers?

  After debating these questions with your friends or classmates, why not try the moral machine again, will you get different results?

Which law has been broken?

- ☑ Consider a range of scenarios: hacking, selling personal data, software piracy, music sampling, disposal of batteries in the domestic waste bin. Explain which law has been broken in each case. Bonus marks for multiple laws or for estimating the sentence correctly!

Link It

Link to networks

The networks and security topics have a lot of overlap with legal and ethical issues. For example, you could adopt the role of an IT manager.

☑ Design an office computer network for a given business, which could be a fast-food restaurant, a hairdressing salon or a solicitor's office. Consider all the impacts and issues of implementing a computer system in the business.

Unplug It

Debate lessons
☑ Ask your teacher to run a class debate, or hold one with your study buddies. Pick a topic:

- The police should be able to read everyone's direct messages.
- Children should be offline until at least the age of 13.
- A carbon tax on smartphones should be introduced to fund recycling.
- Racist algorithms should be banned.

Try to cover many objectives in this topic, such as privacy, ethical, legal, social, environmental and cultural issues. Consider all the relevant stakeholders both now and in the future, such as consumers, workers, vendors, shareholders and the wider society.

AI without computers
☑ You can find an activity called "Paper AI" at the Microsoft MakeCode website for Minecraft (link.httcs.online/paperai). Paul Curzon of Queen Mary, University of London, has published his excellent "Brain in a bag" activity on the Teaching London Computing website (link.httcs.online/braininabug). Many more AI-related activities are available at aiunplugged.org.

Build It

Machine learning for kids and micro:bit cybersecurity
☑ The Raspberry Pi website has activities on the page "Machine learning for kids" at link.httcs.online/pimachinelearning and you'll find micro:bit lessons on cybersecurity and encryption at link.httcs.online/microbitcyber.

Apply It

☑ Google has published lots of activities to help explore machine learning through pictures, drawings, language and music at link.httcs.online/googleai.

Correct It

Misconception	Reality
DPA/GDPR criminalises hacking	The Computer Misuse Act criminalises hacking (unauthorised access)
DPA criminalises piracy	The Copyright, Designs and Patents Act criminalises piracy (unlicensed copying or sharing of intellectual property)
Ethical/legal/cultural/ environmental issue confusion	Ethics are moral principles, or rules, that govern a person's attitudes and behaviour, e.g. public safety. Legal issues pertain to the legality of acts – whether they are against the law or not – e.g. compliance with the DPA. Cultural issues are those that affect the nature and culture of society, e.g. the digital divide or biased algorithms. Environmental issues are those that have an impact on the environment, e.g. teleworking reduces commuting, but e-waste pollutes and causes health issues in developing nations. Some issues overlap: for example, e-waste exports to Africa are illegal and also unethical.
Encryption backdoors "for the good guys only" are possible	Security experts believe encryption backdoors would quickly be found by hackers, rendering the encryption useless.
Cookies steal data or are used for password storage	Cookies cannot access data on hard drives, so cannot read anything; they are plaintext files so would never be used for security data.
Stakeholder/ shareholder/consumer confusion	Stakeholder: any person with a stake, including consumer, vendor, shareholder and society.
Waste phones release CO_2	While waste phones do pose an environmental risk, due to leaching of heavy metals into local water, the carbon impact comes mostly from fossil fuels burned to generate energy for manufacturing replacement phones.
FOI allows individuals to request data held about them	The DPA provides this facility. The Freedom of Information Act gives citizens the right to request information about the activities of public sector bodies.

Misconception	Reality
The digital divide includes software compatibility issues	The digital divide is about disparity of access to technology, not software compatibility.
Young vs old is not digital divide	Young people generally have greater access to technology through familiarity and via the workplace. Young vs old is therefore definitely a digital divide issue.
Creative Commons licensing does not allow onward sharing or derivative works	All CC licences allow resharing. BY-ND and BY-NC-ND do not permit derivatives, i.e. the work cannot be changed. (This knowledge is required by some exam boards only.)

Check It: Issues and impacts

Concept	Need to learn 😧	Getting there 😐	Mastered 😊
I can discuss the issues caused by computing including privacy, legal, ethical, environmental and cultural issues.			
I can define a stakeholder.			
I can describe the legislation relevant to computing including:			
• General Data Protection Regulation (GDPR) and Data Protection Act 2018			
• Computer Misuse Act 1990			
• Copyright, Designs and Patents Act 1988			
• Creative Commons licensing			
• Investigatory Powers Act 2016			
• Freedom of Information Act 2000			
• The "right to be forgotten"			
I can distinguish between creative uses and copyright infringement when making digital content.			
I can explain the digital divide.			
I can name some positive and negative aspects of mobile technology.			
I know the implications of having personal data online.			
I can describe the social and environmental impacts of social media.			
I can name some positive and negative effects of online content.			
I can describe the environmental effects of technology.			
I can discuss the ethical and cultural impacts of AI and algorithms.			

Endnotes

1   Hern, A. (2017) "Facebook translates 'good morning' into 'attack them', leading to arrest", *The Guardian*, link.httcs.online/halawi

2   Larson, J., Mattu, S., Kirchner, L. and Angwin, J. (2016) "How we analyzed the COMPAS recidivism algorithm", ProPublica, link.httcs.online/compas

3   Reynolds, M. (2017) "Biased policing is made word by errors in pre-crime algorithms", *New Scientist*, link.httcs.online/predpol

4   link.httcs.online/liberty

5   Heilweil, R. (2020) "Big tech companies back away from selling facial recognition to police. That's progress", *Vox Recode*, link.httcs.online/facepause

6   link.httcs.online/faceerrors

7   Stokel-Walker, C. (2020) "IBM gives up on face-recognition business ¬– will other firms follow?", *New Scientist*, link.httcs.online/ibmface

8   Fox, B., Gurney, N., Cavestany, M. and van den Dam, R. (2018) *The Trust Factor in the Cognitive Era*, IBM Institute for Business Value, link.httcs.online/ibmtrust

9   Cifas newsroom. (2020) "Cifas reveals cases fo identity fraud up by nearly a third over last five years", link.httcs.online/cifas

10   link.httcs.online/dhhrant

11   Umoja Noble, S. (2018) *Algorithms of Oppression: how search engines reinforce racism*, NYU Press

12   link.httcs.online/googleusage

13   Ekström, A. (2015) "The moral bias behind your search results", TEDxOslo, link.httcs.online/ekstrom

14   Wanjek, C. (2016) "AI boosts cancer screens to nearly 100 percent accuracy", *Live Science*, link.httcs.online/pathai

15   Bresnick, J. (2018) "Healthcare artificial intelligence market to top $34B by 2025", *HealthITAnalytics*, link.httcs.online/healthai

16   BBC News. (2018) "Vote Leave's targeted Brexit ads released by Facebook", link.httcs.online/leaveads

17   Davies, R. and Rushe, D. (2019) "Facebook to pay $5bn fine as regular settles Cambridge Analytica complaint", *The Guardian*, link.httcs.online/facebookfine

18   Yuhas, A. (2017) "'Pizzagate' gunman pleads guilty as conspiracy theorist apologizes over case", *The Guardian*, link.httcs.online/pizzagate

19   Wilson, J. (2019) "Conspiracy theories like QAnon could fuel 'extremist' violence, FBI says", *The Guardian*, link.httcs.online/fbi

20   Amarasingam, A. and Argentino, M-A. (2020) "The AQnon conspiracy theory: a security threat in the making?", *CTC Sentinel*, 13(7), link.httcs.online/ctcqanon

21   Goodman, J. and Carmichael, F. (2020) "Coronavirus: 5G and microchip conspiracies around the world", BBC News, link.httcs.online/5gconspiracy

22   Lee, D. (2018) "The tactics of a Russian troll farm", BBC News, link.httcs.online/russiantrolls

23   Criddle, C. (2021) "Bitcoin consumes 'more electricity than Argentina'", BBC News, link.httcs.online/bitcoinenergy

24   Jones, N. (2018) "How to stop data centres from gobbling up the world's electricity", *Nature*, link.httcs.online/datacentres

25   link.httcs.online/iphoneenergy

26   Forti, V., Baldè, C.P., Kuehr, R., Bellink, G. (2020) *The Global E-waste Monitor 2020: quantities, flows and the circular economy potential*, link.httcs.online/ewaste

27   Wakefield, J. (2016) "Apple, Samsung and Sony face child labour claims", *BBC News*, link.httcs.online/congo

28   Laville, S. (2019) "UK worst offender in Europe for electronic waste exports – report", *The Guardian*, link.httcs.online/ukwaste

29   Bowcott, O. (2020) "Cybercrime laws needs urgent reform to protect UK, says report", *The Guardian*, link.httcs.online/cybercrime

30   Ibid.

31   Fry, H. (2019) *Hello World: how to be human in the age of the machine*, Transworld

32   Leprince-Ringuet, D. (2020) "10 tech predictions that could mean huge changes ahead", *ZDNet*, link.httcs.online/10predictions

33   link.httcs.online/hawkingletter

CHAPTER 12. ASSESS

Let's revisit my AAAA framework for effective study.

Figure 12.1: The four phases of the AAAA framework for effective study

The fourth "A" is "assess". You need to regularly review your progress to stay in control and on track. We will now look at "metacognition" which means thinking about thinking. What's working for you, and what's not? Then we look at exam technique including "command words" and the importance of spelling, punctuation and grammar or "SpAG". Finally some do's and don'ts as exam day approaches. But let's start with going meta...

Metacognition

Metacognition means thinking about your own learning. It's one of three key skills in "self-regulated learning" – taking control of your own study:

- cognition – learning
- metacognition – learning to learn
- motivation – wanting to learn

The Education Endowment Foundation says that metacognition and self-regulation approaches can add seven months additional progress over a school career (see link.httcs.online/eefmeta). So let's take a look at what works:

Talk about learning

The research shows that pupil-to-pupil and pupil-teacher talk can help, so talk about what you are doing with others, as you do it. Work in pairs in the classroom if you are allowed or find a study buddy to do homework with. Explain new concepts to each other. Discuss what strategy you will use to tackle a task. Discuss what went well at the end, and what you would change in the future.

Get feedback

Your teacher should provide timely feedback as often as you need it, make sure you are asking for it if you are stuck or at the end of a task. If you are self-studying or home-schooled then you can use online quizzing tools to check your knowledge, and lots are discussed in chapter 5. Finally, remember your study partner and get them to give you feedback often.

Reflect and assess what worked

I have given you lots of learning tools and tricks in this book, but not everything will be useful to you. We all have our preferences for how we like to learn.

The myth of learning styles

Your school may have done an exercise with you called "learning styles" and defined you as a visual, auditory or kinaesthetic learner. While it's an interesting exercise, and it definitely helps you understand yourself a bit better, research has debunked the VAK model. Like the statements "you only use 10 per cent of your brain" and "listening to Mozart makes you smarter", VAK learning styles are a "neuromyth". In fact, all human brains love to receive information in more than one sensory mode at the same time. Hence you should mix up diagrams with written notes and listen to podcasts and watch tutorials (but not together!), and by all means choreograph an interpretive dance for the bubble sort, but don't believe you have a single "learning style" that you prefer, our brains are infinitely more fascinating and complicated than that!

Learning styles aside, not everything will work for you. Some of my students like to use online quizzes like Smartrevise and Quizlet, others love making mind maps and flashcards. Find out what you like doing, and what helps you remember the stuff. Do more of that!

Stay motivated

We discussed motivation in the Introduction. If you're struggling to get the work done, reassess your motivation. Go back to those career aspirations, that preferred university course, the vision you have of yourself in five years' time. To stay focused on the end goal, print out a picture of your ideal career and stick it above your study space. If you're feeling creative, why not sketch or Photoshop yourself doing your ideal job?

Exam technique

The exams will come whether you are ready or not, so let's talk about them now.

Command words, AOs and number of marks.

Every exam board publishes a list of "command words", the word in an exam question giving an instruction, such as **state, describe**, or **compare**. Knowing these words and what is expected in the answer is very useful in an exam. Knowing the assessment objectives (AOs) and checking the number of marks awarded for a question is also helpful.

Some common command words are listed here. Always check your own exam board's list just to be sure. You can search online for "computer science command words" and the board, e.g. OCR, AQA or Eduqas. Ask your teacher if you are not sure what this is.

Command	Definition
State	Give a specific name, value or other brief answer without explanation or calculation.
Identify	Provide an answer from a number of possibilities. Recognise and state briefly a distinguishing factor or feature.
Explain	Give a detailed account including reasons or causes.
Describe	Give a detailed account or picture of a situation, event, pattern or process.
Discuss	Offer a considered and balanced review that includes a range of arguments, factors or hypotheses. Opinions or conclusions should be presented clearly and supported by appropriate evidence.

Command	Definition
Compare	Give an account of the similarities and differences between two (or more) items or situations, referring to both (or all) of them throughout.
Evaluate	Assess the implications and limitations. Make judgements about the ideas, works, solutions or methods in relation to selected criteria

There are three assessment objectives for computer science:

- AO1: Demonstrate knowledge and understanding
- AO2: Apply knowledge and understanding
- AO3: Analyse problems to make reasoned judgements, design, program, evaluate and refine solutions.

AO1 is "just the facts", but my students sometimes forget the AO1 marks in a longer answer question. For example, when answering a six or nine-mark question about sorting algorithms, lots of AO1 marks are available for simply explaining what a bubble sort is and how it works, before moving on to harder AOs.

When answering a question that is more than two marks long, usually the marks will come from a combination of AO1, 2 and 3. So be ready to hit each of those AOs. Plan your answer on rough paper and tick off the AOs you have covered.

Look at the marks available. Have you written enough to score full marks? For example, to answer a question that says "Describe two methods of translating high level code into machine code [4]" then you need to state two methods (interpreting and compiling) and then for each *describe briefly how it works*, for full marks.

BUG it!

One technique that works for my students is to BUG the question. BUG is the BOX, UNDERLINE, GLANCE technique:

- **Box** – Firstly, box the command word. This highlights what type of answer the examiner is looking for.
- **Underline** – Now underline key words, this jogs your memory of the topic.
- **Glance** – Finally, glance over the question again to gain any more information, making sure you can understand what the examiner is asking you to do. BUG!

---

1. A <u>games developer</u> is developing an online game that can be played on <u>games consoles, desktop computers or mobile phones</u>. The program is written in <u>high-level code</u> and then <u>translated</u> to <u>machine code</u>.

a) Describe two <u>differences</u> between <u>high-level code</u> and <u>machine code</u>.

Figure 12.2: An example of a BUGged question.[1]

Looking at this example, we know we need to **describe** things. That means give an account or description, not just **state** or **identify**. Also we have underlined key words, this is about high and low level languages and translating them. We have also underlined the **games developer** fact because we should refer to the context as we are explaining our answer. We now glance over the question again – have we understood it all? – and start answering.

Practice questions and Smartrevise Advance

For performance in the exam, nothing beats practice. If you get hold of lots of past paper questions, that's great. But I have recommended earlier the excellent "Smartrevise" from Craig 'n' Dave, and this has a practice exam question feature called "Advance". The platform's AI tries to match your answer to the mark scheme, and in this way, you have your own exam marker for self-testing.

And that's it! All the skills you will need to succeed in Computer Science GCSE. Let's wrap up with some background to the book's creation and some further reading.

Endnotes

1   Price, G. and Maier, P. (2007) Effective Study Skills: Essential skills for academic and career success, Longman

CONCLUSION

Aims for this book

My first book, the companion to this entitled *How to Teach Computer Science* was designed to inspire and assist teachers of our thrilling subject. I wrote that book because the first computer science education department was founded at Purdue University, Indiana, in 1962, which gives the academic subject just 60 years of history, and there just wasn't enough written about the subject or how to teach it.

This book was the natural next step, using the research I did for the teacher book, and much of the content, I have created a student book that I hope you find fascinating and inspiring. If your teacher doesn't yet have the first book, then your job is to recommend it to them!

I finished writing the first book *How to Teach Computer Science* in the spring of 2021, and it was warmly received. Craig Sargent and Dave Hillyard (of Craig 'n' Dave fame) were very appreciative but pointed out a big issue, they would love to share the book with their students but it would be a bit odd to give them a book entitled *How to Teach...*! The idea of a student companion was born, and here it is. I tried to include all the advice that I give my students, and everything good in the science of learning today, in an easy to digest form. I hope you find it useful.

Further reading

This book is many things, but it is not a subject textbook. I recommend the digital textbook from Paul Long aimed at schools, and the Isaac Computer Science website. BBC Bitesize remains a brilliant learning resource for all sorts of subjects. For a printed textbook, I like the CGP revision guide and the PGOnline ClearRevise series. For a really riveting read you need to pick up some of these:

- *Code: The Hidden Language of Computer Hardware and Software* by Charles Petzold
- *But How Do It Know? The Basic Principles of Computer for Everyone* – J. Clark Scott
- *Hackers: Heroes of the Computer Revolution* – Steven Levy
- *The Computing Universe: A Journey through a Revolution* – Tony Hey and Gyuri Pápay
- *Hello World: How to be Human in the Age of the Machine* – Hannah Fry

Many more recommended sources including books, podcasts and video channels can be found on my website httcs.online. Just remember, with motivation, self-regulation and all the tricks in this book, you will go far. Don't forget, you're a computer scientist! If you get stuck: use your decomposition skills to break the problem down, solve one piece at a time and always keep moving forward. To give the last word to the great thinker that was Dr. Seuss:

Congratulations!

Today is your day.

You're off to Great Places!

You're off and away!

You have brains in your head.

You have feet in your shoes.

You can steer yourself

any direction you choose.

You're on your own. And you know what you know.

And YOU are the guy who'll decide where to go.[1]

Endnotes

1   Dr. Seuss (1990) *Oh, the Places You'll Go!*, Penguin Random House

ACKNOWLEDGEMENTS

I continue to be impressed by the love and patience shown by my wife Nicola, and I'm unendingly grateful for our two inspirational children. I want to thank my Mam for everything that mothers do (and then some), and to my two late Dads, who always worked two or even three jobs to ensure I never wanted for anything, and could go to university to study computer science in the first place.

After writing this second book, I again want to thank the strategic leadership team at William Hulme's Grammar School in Manchester, and the board of United Learning, for their commitment to professional development

Massive thanks again to Craig Sargent and Dave Hillyard, who you know as Craig 'n' Dave, for their support. They suggested I write this book, then proofread it and wrote the foreword, for which I am hugely grateful. Thanks also to William Lau and Andy Colley for their support, help and expert advice. When such respected educators are so positive about your work, it makes all the effort worthwhile. I hope you enjoy it too.

Alan Harrison, 21 July 2022, Manchester

httcs.online

IMAGE CREDITS

Figure 1.1: Emgravey/CC BY-SA 4.0

Figure 1.2: David Monniaux/CC BY-SA 3.0

Figure 1.5: Mutatis mutandis/CC BY-SA 3.0

Figure 1.6: Russell A. Kirsch/National Institute of Standards and Technology (US)

Figure 2.1: Katie Bouman.

Figure 3.1: AP/Shutterstock.

Figure 3.4: Craig'n'Dave.

Figure 4.1: Massachusetts Institute of Technology (US)

Figure 5.1: Michel Bakni, CC BY-SA 4.0

Figure 6.1: Parrot of Doom/CC BY-SA 3.0

Figure 6.2: Malleus Fatuorum/CC BY 3.0

Figure 6.3: William Lau/CC BY-SA 4.0

Figure 6.4: Tiia Monto/CC BY-SA 3.0

Figure 6.5: Daniel Sancho/CC BY 2.0

Figure 6.6: Peter Howkins/CC BY-SA 3.0

Figure 8.1: Tara Tiger Brown/CC BY-NC-SA 2.0

Figure 8.2: Peter Hamer/Magnus Manske/CC BY-SA 2.0

Figure 8.3: Rezonansowy, Microsoft

Figure 8.4: Sashatemov/Irina Blok/CC0 1.0

Figure 9.1: UCLA/BBN/CC BY-SA 4.0

Figure 9.2: ITU Pictures/CC BY 2.0

Figure 9.3: Robert Scoble/CC BY 2.0

Figure 9.4: Recreated from source: steves-internet-guide.com/internet-protocol-
    suite-explained

Figure 10.3: The National Archives (UK)

Figure 11.1: Prostock-Studio

Figure 11.2: Marlenenapoli/CC0 1.0